DEVOTED
HUSBAND
AND FATHER

JESSE
WOODSON
JAMES

SEPT. 5, 1847
MURDERED
APR. 3, 1882
BY A TRAITOR
AND COWARD
WHOSE NAME
IS NOT WORTHY
TO APPEAR HERE

Haunted
Kansas City
Missouri

Angela Cox

Schiffer Publishing Ltd

4880 Lower Valley Road, Atglen, Pennsylvania 19310

Other Schiffer Books on Related Subjects:
Greetings From St. Louis. Mary L. Martin, Dinah Roseberry & Kim Hufford.
   ISBN: 978-0-7643-2824-4. $24.95
Ghosts of St. Louis: The Lemp Mansion and Other Eerie Tales. Bryan W. Alasap.
   ISBN: 978-0-7643-2688-2. $12.95

**Schiffer Books are available at special discounts for bulk purchases for sales promotions
or premiums. Special editions, including personalized covers, corporate imprints, and ex-
cerpts can be created in large quantities for special needs. For more information contact
the publisher:**
Published by Schiffer Publishing Ltd.
4880 Lower Valley Road
Atglen, PA 19310
Phone: (610) 593-1777; Fax: (610) 593-2002
E-mail: Info@schifferbooks.com
For the largest selection of fine reference books on this and related subjects, please
visit our web site at **www.schifferbooks.com** We are always looking for people to write
books on new and related subjects. If you have an idea for a book please contact us at the
above address.

This book may be purchased from the publisher.
Include $5.00 for shipping.
Please try your bookstore first.
You may write for a free catalog.
In Europe, Schiffer books are distributed by
Bushwood Books
6 Marksbury Ave.
Kew Gardens
Surrey TW9 4JF England
Phone: 44 (0) 20 8392-8585; Fax: 44 (0) 20 8392-9876
E-mail: info@bushwoodbooks.co.uk
Website: www.bushwoodbooks.co.uk
Free postage in the U.K., Europe; air mail at cost.

Cover photo: Snowfall on the plaza, Kansas City, Mo. with the plaza lights and bench ©
Michael Bailey. This image is from Big Stock Photos.com.
Designed by Stephanie Daugherty
Type set in a Theme for murder/Rosemary Roman/Bergell LET/Dutch809 BT/BrushScript
BT/Smudger Alts LET

ISBN: 978-0-7643-3194-7
Printed in the United States of America

Dedication

This book is for Aaron and Dante and Lauren.

The idea of death, the fear of it,

haunts the human animal like nothing else;

it is a mainspring of human activity -

designed largely to avoid the fatality of death,

to overcome it by denying in some way

that it is the final destiny of man."

—Ernest Becker

Disclaimer: This book is a compilation of real ghost stories from around the Kansas City area. Many of the stories about historic landmarks in this region are rooted in local lore and legend, but all were related to me personally through interviews and casual discussions. I have attempted to weave in historical facts and truisms with the legends, but as with any good ghost story passed down through the years, some of them seem to get better with the telling. As such, we must keep in mind that there often is a fine line between fact and fiction, which doesn't diminish our enjoyment of the tale.

Other stories included in this book are highly individualized experiences that real people have unselfishly shared. I thank them for their willingness to talk with me so candidly.

All of the places described in this book exist. If the urge strikes you, the reader, to go ghost hunting in any of these locations, please remember to respect the people living, working, or learning there. Never trespass on private property and always get permission to visit any place after hours.

Contents

Acknowledgements

For ideas, suggestions, and contributions to this work, I thank the people mentioned in the text by name, as well as those who told me stories anonymously.

Paul and Pat Cummings, in addition to being great parents, were indispensable as my super-powered editing team, ghost-hunting chauffeurs, and all-around good guys. Rich and Melissa King were generous enough to share their spooky anecdotes and wealth of information regarding Kansas City ghost legends. Thanks to Lance Cox for his ghoulish connections and supernatural accounts. My editor at Schiffer, Dinah Roseberry, gave me unequaled editorial advice and guidance. Her patience with all of my questions and concerns was certainly appreciated.

For providing the moral support and listening ear I needed during numerous meltdowns, I would like to thank the following wonderful people: Diane Migletz, Pam Weis, Karen Colwell, and Kim Cates. My siblings deserve credit for all the terrifying stories and nighttime adventures we shared as youngsters, as well as my nieces and nephews who are carrying on the tradition!

Last, but not least, I want to thank my children, Lauren and Dante, for my special 'Ghost Story' notebook and pen that helped me stay motivated to the very end. And to Aaron, I just say, "Thank you." There is no way I could have researched, written, and photographed this book without him.

Preface

My fascination with all things spooky—ghosts, spirits, scary stories, began at an early age. My birthday is on October 31st, and so I wonder if it could have ever been otherwise.

I grew up on a livestock farm just north of Kansas City and it was there where I experienced my first other-worldly encounter. It was a cold winter evening, well past midnight. I had tagged along with my father to check on a mother pig ready to give birth. We had driven the old blue Ford pickup out to the back 40 acres of the farm and it was bitterly cold--one of those chilly, beautifully clear winter nights we get in the Midwest that I love so much. The two of us were totally alone in the very back part of our farmland—just my father and me.

We parked the truck and began looking in the long low-hung tin barn for the mother pig when I felt a prickling along my neck. I looked around me, but there was nothing to see but darkness. Yet the eerie feeling lingered. It was like there was someone standing inside the barn with us. I had been aiming my flashlight at the ground so that I wouldn't trip and remember gripping it tighter as fear coiled inside me. I franticly aimed the light into all of the corners of the barn (earning me a strange look from my father) but found nothing out of the ordinary. There was nothing that my eyes could see except dust and a few old 2x4s. I asked Dad if he thought there was anyone in the barn with us. He patiently looked around and assured me that there was nothing to be afraid of out there.

Eventually, we found the mother and her healthy piglets and went back home. From an outside point of view, everything appeared normal. My view of the world, however, was changed. It was out on a remote parcel of land in the dead of winter that I first came to realize that spirits and ghosts do exist if only we are open to 'seeing' or feeling them.

My second experience came not quite a year later in that very same blue Ford truck. My parents, younger siblings, and I were on our way home from Atchison, Kansas where we had attended a livestock auction. We were getting sleepy, but our parents decided to take a 'shortcut.' Actually, they thought it would be funny if they scared the pants off us. At a bend in the road, my father slowed the truck and pulled carefully onto a gravel road. He put the truck into park and then turned off the lights. There was no moon out and we were enveloped in pitch blackness. The hot summer night was

Just one of many spooky country lanes found around Kansas City.

filled with the chorus of June bugs until my mother began to tell us what we knew was going to be a very scary story. Just then, I felt a prickling sense that there was a presence just outside the truck and in the woods. It was not a vague feeling of eeriness. I was down-right scared and asked Mom to stop her story. My younger sisters were extremely spooked and started yelling loudly for Dad to drive away. I'm not sure if they felt the same malicious spirit I did, or if the darkness was too much for them. Regardless, we were all yelling for them to just drive, and so my parents turned the lights back on and we went on home. The story they finished telling me the next day—what had happened in the very spot we had pulled into, is included in this book. It is the story of Murder and Injustice.

From then on, I read every ghost story book I could get my hands on. If the story was combined with history, then so much the better. My two younger sisters and I would often stay up late in our room telling stories sure to keep us awake well past our bedtime. My family's many games of hide and seek in the dark also served to solidify my comfort with the night. Don't get me wrong, I go through stages where I need the lights ON! There were a couple of times when writing this book, in fact, when I jumped out of my skin because one of my own children crept up on me and set my heart to beating rapidly! What is it about the nighttime that raises our awareness of ethereal spirits? It is something indefinable and mysterious that makes us wonder what else is out there.

What you will find here is a compilation of otherworldly tales and experiences from the Kansas City area—primarily on the Missouri side of the border. Kansas City has such a wonderfully varied past, it only makes sense that its ghostly history reflects that diversity.

Having been born and raised in 'The City of Fountains,' I was already quite familiar with many of the historical ghost stories associated with well-known landmarks. I researched background information where needed and have tried to provide you, the reader, with a full picture. Other stories included in this book are personal experiences that folks so wonderfully shared with me. I apologize to these good people for any mistakes I may have inadvertently made in the retelling.

In addition to jazz, barbeque, and farming, Kansas City is also well-known for its haunted houses--staged Haunted Houses that you pay to visit during the Halloween season. As a child, my family (four sisters and one brother) would pile in the car and go to the small, community-based haunted houses on at least one night during the Halloween season. As a teenager, my need for fright increased dramatically, and so my friends and I would visit the big haunted houses that are scattered all around downtown Kansas City beginning in September each year. If you are in town during this amazing time, you should really check it out. There are several well-established haunted houses that have been around for more than twenty years and know how to give a good fright! What is it about getting scared, but knowing you won't be harmed, that is so very attractive? I think that is why ghost stories are so much fun. We can get all of the excitement without any of the danger as we stay tucked safely into our favorite chair at home.

This book contains many spooky stories about haunted places and unexplainable occurrences in Kansas City. Some stories, such as the ghost of Betsy Ward at the Savoy Hotel, may be familiar to you. Other tales, like the Whistling Stranger will be new, but just as alarming. Stories about apparitions and spirits from all throughout Kansas City's varied history can be found here. Civil War heroes and outlaws, Prohibition flappers, and Depression-era gangsters are all represented. From long ago clear to the present, numerous stories are told about restless spirits lingering within this wonderful city. I hope you enjoy reading the stories retold here as much as I have enjoyed compiling them.

1

The Hook

Following is one of my favorite ghost stories. I do not know the origin of it and can only imagine that kids everywhere have a similar version placed in their hometown. My family's version has the location as a back road in rural Missouri.

Emily and Luke decided to take a detour on the way home from the movies one Saturday night. It was an unseasonably warm autumn night and they had time to spare before their curfews arrived. Luke pulled onto a country lane and parked his pickup truck along the edge of a pasture. The two teenagers cuddled close in the front seat and looked out into the night. They talked about whatever entered their heads. Homecoming was the next weekend and they excitedly outlined their big plans for the evening's festivities. Suddenly, Emily stopped talking and tilted her head to one side. "Do you hear that?" she asked Luke. Luke listened closely and was able to hear the sound about which Emily was talking.

"Scratch, scratch, scratch!"

At first the sound was faint, but soon it gained volume. Again, they heard "Scratch! Scratch! Scratch!" This time, however, it sounded like it was coming from on top of the cab of the truck! Emily shivered and moved closer to Luke. "Do you think it's a tree branch scraping the top of the truck?" she whispered. Luke looked around and saw that there weren't any trees close to them. "I don't know. I don't think so," he responded.

Luke put the key in the ignition and rolled down his window the rest of the way. Leaning his head out, he looked all around and on top of the vehicle. He couldn't see anything that would be causing the sound. Just as he sat back in his seat, the couple heard the most frightening sound of all. "Scraaaaatch!" A long scraping sound started on the roof above Luke's head and moved all the way across to Emily's side. A tree branch could **not** have made that sound. The teenagers didn't waste a moment more. Luke threw the truck into drive and sped away from the area as fast as his pickup could go.

When they arrived back at Emily's house, they sprinted from the truck and into her home as if being chased by demons. Needing no persuasion, they told Emily's parents what had happened. Together, the group opened the garage door and turned on the outside lights to have a look at the pickup. What they saw shocked them to the core.

On the roof of the cab were a series of scrape marks gouged deep into the paint and metal. No tree branch could have made those marks. It appeared as if a hook of some kind had been used in an attempt to break into the truck. But Luke had looked out and seen nothing. What had caused those marks and for what reason? Luke and Emily feel certain that whatever it was, it intended to do them harm and they never returned to that lonely country lane again.

Harvey House

(A Professor's Legacy)

The young couple, Carolyn and James, had just returned from their honeymoon full of energy and excitement—looking forward to moving into their new home in Liberty, Missouri. They were soon settled and Carolyn found that she loved the house even though she could hear strange noises and loud creaking as she rested in bed at night. It was more than a little eerie, but the house had a history and a story and she longed to bring it back to its former glory.

Carolyn's father-in-law, James Carmichael, had purchased the house earlier that summer at auction from William Jewell College for a mere $6,000. The previous owner had been an English professor at the nearby college. His name was P. Casper Harvey, and upon his death had bequeathed his home to the college that he had loved so much.

There is no apparent connection between P. Casper Harvey-- the English professor, and Harvey Productions--producers of the old Casper the Friendly Ghost cartoons from the 60s. But what a remarkable coincidence!

Mr. Carmichael was interested in the old place because he (as well as many other family members) had graduated from William Jewell. Professor Harvey had been one of his favorite educators there. After purchasing the home, he told his son and daughter-in-law that they could stay in the house if they would help to refinish it. It was a big job, however, since the place had become quite neglected over the years.

Carolyn remembers a terrible green décor throughout the home that definitely needed replacing. And the place had some odd characteristics. There was a door inside a walk-in closet that opened to a wall. Even though it was most likely due to various additions to the home, it was still a little strange. The screened-in back porch was jammed full with old papers and office supplies from Professor Harvey's teaching days. While clearing it out, Carolyn and family found student papers written in the 1920s and 30s. The family gathered the relics together and gave them to Clay County since they did not want to just throw them away. As the clutter of decades was slowly cleared away, Carolyn could finally imagine the modest one-story house as a true Victorian home filled with antiques and other period pieces. What she did not envision was the ghost they unveiled during the restoration process!

At first, the couple thought they were simply losing or misplacing small items. It was a hectic time and they did not give the incidents much thought. Eventually, however, items began to vanish almost right before their eyes. They would put something on a table, walk out of the room, and upon their return the item would be gone!

Harvey House in downtown Liberty, Missouri, home to the ghost of a William Jewell College professor and his wife.

Doors would shut by themselves and the couple often heard floor-boards creaking under the weight of an unseen person. From time to time, they would catch a glimpse of a figure out of the corner of their eye. They never saw a clearly defined apparition, but always seemed to catch the spirit floating away from them. The burners on an old gas stove in the kitchen would shut off by themselves. Carolyn and James tried to play off the strange occurrences by reminding themselves that it was an old house and bound to have its idiosyncrasies. But something or someone in the house obviously wanted their attention and simply kept trying harder and harder to get it!

James was a police officer and every night, he would place his gun belt in the same location under the bed. Several times over the course of a few months, James' gun belt would be moved slightly from its location, but not enough to cause uneasiness. James simply thought that he had moved it with his foot in the night or chalked it up to some other reasonable explanation. But one morning upon awakening, James discovered that his gun belt had been moved all the way into the kitchen and onto the breakfast table. He knew he had placed it in its usual spot under the bed the night before. Carolyn assured him that she had not touched it. So what could have caused such an important item to be moved so far from where it belonged?

All of these unexplainable happenings spooked the Carmichael family, but since they never felt threatened in any way, they were also quite intrigued. They were never scared, for the activities of their resident spirit were always kind—more like ghostly pranks. They thought that maybe the spirit responsible just wanted them to acknowledge his or her presence. So the couple decided to look into the previous owners a little further.

According to their research, Professor Harvey was married to a woman named Virginia and they had no children together. They appeared to be upright citizens, attending the Christian Church on Sundays, and being active in the community. Virginia was known to be very prim and proper—always wearing a hat and long white gloves. Their research led the Carmichaels to believe that the ghosts in the Harvey house were happy to have occupants that were able to bring their home back to the way Virginia had always wanted it to be. Apparently, Mr. Harvey was a bit of a spendthrift so the house became a mishmash of repairs and additions, much to the frustration of his wife.

After Carolyn and James moved out, other family members tried to stay there from time to time but were too alarmed by the ghostly happenings to stay for long. Carolyn's mother-in-law said she always felt a presence in the house with her and was frightened by it.

3

The Cats

Following is one particular interaction with the ghost of Harvey House that stands out as the most bizarre of all the Carmichaels' experiences there.

Throughout their tenure in Harvey House, the Carmichaels had noticed that a neighbor was mistreating his cat—leaving it out in the cold, kicking it, not feeding it. One day, while on the way to the grocery store, Carolyn and James saw their opportunity to save this ill-treated animal. The cat was all alone in the street. Its hair was matted and the poor thing just looked terrible. The couple picked it up and took it straight to the veterinarian's office. The vet treated it for fleas, shaved its head and paws, and helped clean it up. He suggested that for a few days, the Carmichaels should keep it separate from their own beloved cat, Brandy Rae.

So when they returned home, they placed the newly rescued cat (looking pretty funky with its shaved body parts) out on their screened-in back porch so that it could get some fresh air, but remain separate. They then put Brandy Rae in the bathroom and closed the door firmly. (They did not turn the old-fashioned skeleton key to lock it because there was no reason to. It was just a cat!) Then they went to finish their original errand at the store.

When they returned, Carolyn and James went to the bathroom to let Brandy Rae out and could not have been more surprised at what they found. Instead of their beloved family feline, Brandy Rae, they found a cat with a shaved head and paws! Of course, when they checked the screened-in back porch, there sat Brandy Rae looking at them as if nothing at all crazy had just happened. No one but the couple had been in the house all day long. There was no way the two cats could have switched places unless they had had some help—most likely from P. Casper Harvey!

Through all of the strange incidents and brushes with things otherworldly in the house, James and Carolyn never once felt threatened or scared. Freaked out at times? Absolutely. Once they acknowledged that they apparently shared their home with the spirits of its previous owners, however, they were able to relax and more readily dealt with the little 'surprises' that came their way.

4

The Farm Home of the Outlaw Jesse James

On my very first visit to the James Farm, I had an extremely unexpected experience. Eight or so visitors were standing in the main living room of the small log cabin exhibit. Our tour guide was informing us that just above our heads existed a four-foot high crawl space where the James children used to sleep. She explained how the children did not spend much time there during the day and only went up at bedtime. As she spoke, she reached to open the closet which contained steps leading up to that attic space. As soon as she turned the handle, we heard a startling sound move across the ceiling above our very heads. "Thud, Thud, Thud!"

Everyone jumped in surprise and then nervous laughter broke out amongst the touring guests. Was it a ghost from the past? Had we surprised Jesse or his brother Frank hiding out from lawmen in the attic of their mother's home? Not this time. The guide explained that it was most likely a raccoon who had taken up residence in the attic of the small farm structure—a staff member had seen it the day before. But the incident did bring to mind, however, some of the strange occurrences I had heard about at the Jesse James Farm Home.

Following is a personal experience our tour guide, Beth, related to me that day. This time, she did not have a reasonable explanation for what happened to her.

Beth unlocked the side door of the old farm home and prepared for the upcoming tour. It was not the first tour she had given of

The farm Home of Jesse James in Kearney, Missouri, is possibly the oldest standing home in Clay County.

the boyhood home of Jesse James, but it would be the last that day. The sun was starting to dip below the horizon, the fading light making it harder to see what she was doing. The group waiting outside the front door was in good spirits and seemed likely to ask lots of questions. She silently rehearsed the facts and stories that accompanied her tour.

As she unlocked the door and began to enter the old homestead, she was stopped dead in her tracks by the sound of steady, but quick footsteps moving across the room and away from the very door she had just opened! They were heavy and sounded as if the person was wearing boots of some sort because they had made a distinct clomping sound on the wooden floor. Her heart beat faster. Was it a vagrant seeking shelter or someone who had broken in to loot the contents of the house? Maybe it was a thrill-seeker sneaking into the old log cabin, wanting to face the memories of so many past lives in the dark.

The guide listened for the sound of the back door opening, hoping the intruder would let himself out just as he'd let himself in. But that sound did not come. No doors opened or closed. She

The two front rooms of the James home were mail-ordered from a Sears catalog.

caught her breath and decided it was just her imagination--her mind playing tricks on her in the dusk. Beth squared her shoulders and stepped firmly through the threshold and into the little room. As she moved toward the front door, she saw nothing but the familiar artifacts left in the house. No one was hiding. No other tour guides jumped out to scare her and laugh. The ring of the heavy, booted footsteps hung hauntingly in her mind.

When she reached the front door in the newer part of the house to let in the next group of tourists, she was a little unsettled and thought maybe she had just imagined the sound. However, the group exclaimed that they had also heard the footfall across the wooden planks and expected someone to jump out and scare them! Maybe she wasn't imagining it after all.

Are there ghostly emanations from the past inhabiting the childhood home of the infamous outlaw Jesse James? Some say most definitely "yes." For more than a century, lingering spirits have been said to make themselves known in this small, rural home 25 minutes outside Kansas City, Missouri. The Jesse James Farm Home and Museum is located at 21216 James Farm Road near Kearney, Missouri and guided tours are given regularly during operating hours.

Residents in the area, as well as staff, have seen lights blinking on and off long after the site is closed for the night. Guests have reported seeing movement in the surrounding woods. When these events are followed up on, no reasonable explanation is found. Upon entering the home, I sensed that there was an other-worldly presence there. I felt like I was stepping into another time and place and could imagine the James clan coming and going. Others have reported hearing voices speaking quietly as well as hearing the nickering of horses and rustling of something moving about in the brush. Who could be responsible for the strange occurrences in what may be the oldest standing structure in Clay County? For that answer, we must understand the history of the location a little better.

The little log cabin was built in 1822 and purchased by a Baptist minister, Reverend Robert James, and his wife Zerelda in 1845. The house came with 205 acres of rich farmland. Their son Frank was two years old at the time. On September 5, 1847, Jesse Woodson James was born in the log cabin, followed two years later by his sister, Susan James.

The woods surrounding the James home may be haunted. Visitors and staff report hearing the unexplainable sounds of horses nickering and voices speaking in low tones.

Reverend James was active and well-respected in the community. He helped establish William Jewell College, an institution that still exists today in nearby Liberty, Missouri. However, the Reverend's time in Missouri was short-lived. On April 12, 1850, he left his young family to go to California and preach in the gold rush camps. Shortly thereafter, on Aug. 18, 1850, Reverend Robert James died of cholera in a Placerville, California gold camp. His wife and three children, left behind on the farm, were destitute.

Two years later, on September 30, 1852, Zerelda married Benjamin Simms, a well to-do neighbor. It was said that the marriage was not a happy one as Simms would not allow the James children to live with them and may have even dealt with them unkindly. Zerelda filed for divorce, but Simms died of a fall from his horse before it was final on January 2, 1854. Because of the laws of the time, Zerelda received nothing from his estate. She and her children were left penniless once more.

A little while later, on September 25, 1855, Zerelda married Dr. Archie Rueben Samuel. This time, she signed a prenuptial agreement before marriage, but as it turns out never needed it. Samuel was a well-educated, soft-spoken man—a good complement to the outspoken and 'larger-than-life' Zerelda. This match would last more than 50 years.

About this time, most families in Missouri were trying to stay out of the Civil War, not siding with either the North or the South. The James/Samuel family did keep slaves but the number was small--not enough to drag them into the conflict. Soon, however, the Civil War invaded the beautiful countryside with its rolling hills and rich pastures and brought with it anger and violence. It changed, forever, the lives on the James/Samuel family farm.

On May 4, 1861, at the age of 18, Frank joined the Confederate army. After his discharge, he joined a band of fighters called William Quantrill's Raiders. It is purported that Frank was among Quantrill's men when they led a raid on Lawrence, Kansas, a nearby Free-State town. More than 180 men, women, and children were killed in the massacre.

In 1863, a group of Union militiamen came to the James farm looking for Frank and other members of the Quantrill Raiders. When their whereabouts were not disclosed, the Union soldiers tortured Dr. Samuel by hanging him repeatedly from a large tree outside his home. This torture is credited as the cause of some mental incapacity suffered by Mr. Samuel. He lived his final days in an asylum in St. Joseph, Missouri. When they still had not found the information they desired, the Union men found the adolescent Jesse out in the fields. They beat him in an unsuccessful effort to extract information on the whereabouts of the Quantrill raiders and his brother, Frank.

That was probably the starting point for the violent and turbulently short life of Jesse James. The next year, 1864, Jesse joined William "Bloody Bill" Anderson's guerilla forces at the age of 16.

When the Civil War ended, the James brothers shifted their activities to robbery. On February 13, 1866, Jesse and Frank James, along with Cole and Jim Younger and nine other members of the gang, robbed the Clay County Savings Bank in Liberty, Missouri (about 15 miles south of Kearney). They came away with $62,000, but it was not taken cleanly. As they were leaving the bank a 17 year-old boy was killed. This was the first daytime robbery of any U.S. bank during peacetime. That bank still stands today and a realistic reenactment of the robbery is performed each summer at the Liberty festival.

For more than ten years after the end of the war, Jesse's gang of outlaws stole from banks, trains, and stagecoaches throughout the Midwest. Many idealized the James brothers' activities as being aimed solely against Union members and supporters. In reality, they simply stole what they could and used the proceeds to support their own families. The Robin Hood image was mostly facilitated by John Newman Edwards' glorifying articles and dime-store novels sensationalizing Frank and Jesse's exploits. He made their thefts seem like wild adventures and the nation was enthralled. Of the two brothers, Jesse had a charisma and easy-going air about him that drew people to him more so than Frank, hence his greater popularity.

While their spoils may have gone to help feed their families, they also put those same family members' lives and general well-being in jeopardy. Similar to the incident that occurred when Jesse was a young man, lawmen were always approaching his childhood home where his mother and family still lived looking for the brothers. Sometimes these 'visits' had terrible consequences. The most notorious example, and one that most likely turned the tide of (or at least solidified) popular opinion in the James family's direction, was the Pinkerton raid on the farmhouse in January 25, 1875.

For years, the famous Pinkerton detective agency had been on the trail of the James brothers. The brothers, however, always seemed to be one step ahead and the detectives were getting frustrated. Eventually, they were able to engage a neighbor to spy for them. When that spy reported to Pinkerton detectives that they saw two men and their horses approach the homestead and remain there, the detectives thought they finally had the James brothers in their sights. That night, six men surrounded the log home and waited until midnight to make their move.

In an effort to smoke out the occupants inside, they tried to light one wall of the house on fire. Unfortunately, it had snowed the night before and the wall would not light. So they lit and threw a smoke bomb through the kitchen window. There were many people in the kitchen at the time including Jesse's mother, step-father, and their son Archie, nine years old. When the smoke bomb came in through the window, Mr. Samuel swept it into the fireplace thinking it was going to catch the house on fire. However, due to the make-up of the bomb, the coals from the fireplace heated it up beyond its capacity and it exploded in the little room. Fragments hit Zerelda, Jesse's mother, in the arm and Archie in the stomach. Archie died the next day and Zerelda's arm was damaged so badly it had to be amputated at the elbow. The James brothers were not at the farm and the raid had been for nothing.

Back view of the oldest portion of the James farm homestead. The window seen in the exposed area leads to the kitchen. Through it, Pinkerton agents tossed the smoke bomb that killed Jesse's half-brother and injured his mother.

A note on family loyalty from the James family: Two weeks after the Pinkerton raid, the neighbor who had worked as a spy for the Pinkerton agents was found shot to death in front of his house. Some people say that while the brothers may not have been home at the time of the raid, they most likely arrived home two weeks later...

The nefarious activities of the James gang continued for many more years until on April 3, 1882, Jesse James was murdered by a member of his own gang. Robert Ford and his brother, Charles, had been visiting at Jesse's home in St. Joseph, Missouri. Jesse, in a rare moment without his guns, stepped up on a stool to straighten and dust a picture on the wall. Ford shot him in the back of his head, just below his right ear, killing him instantly.

After much publicity surrounding his death, Jesse was returned to the James family farm for burial. Zerelda insisted he be buried near her home so that she could keep an eye out for grave robbers and curiosity-seekers. In 1902, Jesse's body was moved to the Mount Olivet Cemetery in Kearney to lie next to his wife, Zee. There, it did not take long for souvenir hunters to chip away at his gravestone leaving nothing but the base.

Original gravesite of Jesse James next to his childhood home. In later years, the pebbles covering the grave were sold to visitors as souvenirs.

The inscription on Jesse James' tombstone was written by his unforgiving mother: "Devoted husband and father Jesse Woodson James. Murdered April 3, 1882 by a traitor and coward whose name is not worthy to appear here."

In later years, Zerelda began running tours of the log cabin where her son Jesse was born and laid to rest. Visitors could buy pebbles off of Jesse's grave for a quarter. When she ran out, Zerelda simply replenished her supply with pebbles from the creek down the hill from the house. Eventually, Frank took over the tours at the log cabin and included a stop at his beloved horse's grave site as well. No one now knows precisely where that original grave is located because Frank kept moving the marker closer and closer to the house as his health deteriorated.

The farm remained in the James family until 1978 when the Clay County Historical Society purchased it from Jesse's grandchildren and restoration efforts began.

The James farm is listed as an Historic Landmark by the Clay County Historical Society.

The porch leads off the original two-room log cabin that Jesse James called home. Some of the original lumber shows how it may have looked when Jesse lived there.

Long-time residents in the area have always heard that the James Farm Home was haunted. It seems that there's enough history here to support a whole cast of spirits from the past. So who haunts the farm--flickering lights and holding hushed conversations? It is estimated that the 200 acres are littered with untold stories and bodies in unmarked graves. It could be outlaws, lawmen, family members or neighbors; siblings, offspring, slaves (or 'workers' as Zerelda liked to call them), and their families. It could even be souls lost while passing through to the west before the house was built; before the James clan even existed. It is hard to say.

Maybe if we sat long enough on the porch of the old log cabin with the light of day fading, we would hear the sounds and see the lights so often mentioned. Maybe Jesse or Frank or Zerelda would sit next to us and share their stories with us.

5

Hide and Seek

I
t was a beautiful fall night—warm enough to wear a sweatshirt and shorts, but cold enough to burn your throat when you started running around. The four college students were playing hide and seek in a four-block radius in downtown Maryville, Missouri. The moon was lighting the streets pretty well, but it was still scary and exciting because they were playing in the empty streets at night! Everyone was on their own—so if someone found a good spot, they had to wait all by themselves for whomever was 'it' to find them.

The nighttime sounds of the sleepy town were a little creepy as Sue waited all alone in the dark. Maryville is an old town with beautiful trees lining many of the streets. She had climbed up in one that had a relatively low branch and felt confident she was not going to be found for quite some time. As Sue sat crouched in her arboreal hiding spot, she heard a variety of noises. Many were the ordinary nocturnal noises like small animals and squirrels foraging around in the fallen leaves. But soon she heard something that made her heart beat faster and goose bumps to appear on her arms.

Directly below her, Sue heard whispering voices. It sounded like several different people all whispering at once. They were talking quickly, almost fervently. The words were indistinguishable, but particularly unsettling and strange. Even though Maryville is an extremely safe college town, Sue initially feared for her well-being. Was a group of rowdy college students passing by from the bar down the street? Or was it a bunch of kids up to some mischief? She peered down from her lofty position but saw no one anywhere near the tree where she was hiding. In fact, she didn't see anyone up or down the street. Without warning the whispering ceased, and

Sue once again heard only the ordinary nocturnal sounds of a sleepy town. Thinking she should find her friends, Sue jumped down to the ground and looked around. There was still no one out that she could see, and the whispering voices never returned.

Sue almost wished that she had seen a group of kids messing around because then she would have had a reasonable explanation for the urgent whispers. Had Sue heard a group of kids on the next block over—their voices somehow carried over to her on the wind? Or were the secret whispers in the dark those from spirits long since gone from the world of the living?

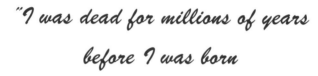

"I was dead for millions of years

before I was born

and it never inconvenienced me a bit."

—Mark Twain

6

Epperson House

at the University of Missouri, Kansas City

Why do ghost stories swirl around educational institutions like leaves in a tornado? I believe it is because so much takes place in a relatively small space—stories which are happy, sad, funny, and bizarre. So many complex interactions occur in the huge melting pot of college campuses that strange experiences are sure to happen. Plus, urban legends and lore abound where fertile young minds gather-- sharing stories and telling tales. Following are but a few examples of haunted college campuses around the Kansas City area.

The security officer was performing a security check around the grounds of the Epperson House on the campus of UMKC when he was suddenly rear-ended. His car was stopped along the side of the house when he felt something crash forcefully into the back of it. The sound of shattering glass was loud in the dark night.

Looking in his rearview mirror, he saw nothing but the night sky. So he grabbed his flashlight and got out of the car to investigate what might have hit him. The security officer walked to the back of his vehicle, but there was nothing behind him--no car, nothing. Mysteriously, there was no damage to his car either; his bumper was not dented and there was no broken glass littering the ground as he expected. There were, however, eight inches of skid marks on the street directly under his tires. His car had unexplainably been knocked forward by some unseen force. This story, cited in an article in the *Kansas City Star* in May 1979, is only one of many stories surrounding the beautiful Tudor-style mansion that sits towering over the south end of 52nd street between Cherry and Oak streets.

Epperson House sits majestically on a hill on the campus of UMKC. Hosting an intricate collection of secret passageways, trapdoors, and tunnels, this mansion is the setting for numerous mysterious occurrences.

The mansion is surrounded by oak and elm trees which earned this house its name of "Hawthorne Hall." During its construction in the early 1920s, Mrs. Elizabeth Epperson referred to it as "Epperson's Folly." The $450,000 project was ambitious to say the least. Uriah Spray Epperson, insurance tycoon and philanthropist, designed the four story mansion with 48 rooms, six baths, an elevator, swimming pool, and billiards room. Interestingly, the house was built with an intricate set of secret passageways, tunnels, and trapdoors all throughout its living spaces. The mystique that surrounds the home earned Epperson House an appearance on "Unsolved Mysteries" as one of the top five haunted houses in the country.

Over the years, many strange and ghostly incidents have been reported here. It is said that just after Mrs. Epperson died in 1939, the empty house (Uriah had passed in 1927) was used as housing for hundreds of Air Corps cadets who needed a transitional place to stay during WWII deployments. These men soon began telling tales of a piano played by unseen hands; the haunting music heard at odd times during the night.

In 1942, Epperson House was donated to the University and was first used as a men's dormitory. Almost 15 years later, it housed the School of Education and was later turned into the Student Center. Through the years, the stately mansion was used by a variety of groups. The Music Department used it in the 1970s and stories of music coming from rooms that did not have a piano began to surface again. Some stories told of

Unexplained footsteps have been heard and an apparition of a women in a long flowing dress has been seen (among many other eerie incidents) inside this beautiful old mansion, Epperson House.

organ music being played in the vicinity of the basement pool. Students claimed to have seen the apparition of a woman in a long evening gown floating on one stairway. Some reported that she was singing and that they could hear her voice. Others believed her to be crying.

Security guards have reported hearing footsteps along the hallways among other mysterious incidents. One involved two security guards performing a routine walk-through of the house after hours. Entering each room, they would flip the light on, look around, and then switch it off again. In one particular room, the light switch would not turn off. They tried several times with no success. As they hesitated just outside the room to make a note to inform maintenance of the problem, they noticed an arm, clothed in a blue suit, reach out and fumble with the switch. The room was immediately engulfed in darkness.

Now home to UMKC's Department of Architectural Studies, Epperson House accommodates classrooms and design studios. One student reported that while staying late in the studio one night, he heard footsteps just outside the door. When no one appeared, he brushed it off as his imagination. But when he heard footsteps again on the floor directly above where he was working, he thought it was time to leave! Another student reported while working alone in the studio, all the open windows suddenly banged shut! It was a warm, calm night and it did not seem possible that a gust of wind could have closed several windows all at once. The student made no pretense at staying a moment longer in Epperson House that night and she made a hasty exit.

So who is responsible for the supernatural occurrences at Epperson House? Many believe that the spirit of Harriet Evelyn Barse is to blame. She moved in with the Eppersons just after her mother died and was referred to as their 'adopted' daughter, even though she was 10 years the senior of Mrs. Epperson. A music lover, Harriet designed a massive pipe organ created for the loft in the 48 ft living room. The room also contained a stage intended for plays and various performances. Before the organ was completed, Harriet died of supposed complications from a gall bladder operation. Oddly, no obituary was placed in the paper. Amid the mysterious details surrounding the death, it was speculated that Harriet actually died after a poorly executed in-home abortion. Rumors flew that she was involved with the hired help and that those who knew her were trying to keep the news quiet. No data has proven any of those theories. An autopsy was never performed to confirm cause of death.

Despite the circumstances that surrounded her passing, many believe the tragic end of Harriet's life has caused her spirit to remain in Epperson House.

7

The Playhouse

at the University of Missouri, Kansas City

A UMKC student related this story of the haunted Playhouse on campus.

Actors and actresses have reported feeling an eerie presence on the stage with them at The Playhouse. Local lore points to the ghost of a woman who died in the playhouse in the late 1950s. She died in the arms of the stage manager and now she remains to walk the stage in her afterlife. People who work in the playhouse have reported hearing unexplained footsteps along the halls and feeling cold spots backstage.

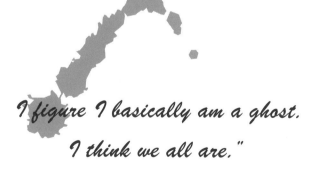

I figure I basically am a ghost.
I think we all are."

—John Astin

8

Roberta Hall

at Northwest Missouri State University

Northwest Missouri State University, 90 miles north of Kansas City in Maryville, Missouri, has one ghost story that just about every new student hears at one time or another. It is associated with one of the girl's dormitories on campus.

In the 1950s, a girl named Roberta Steele was living in the dormitories at Northwest when a terrible accident occurred. A gas tank exploded and flew into the dormitory next to it. Flames from the explosion could be seen clear across town and from out in the countryside. Roberta was critically injured in the explosion and died some time later from her injuries.

Eventually, a new dormitory was named after her and students living in Roberta Hall have many stories to tell. Windows open and close; doors lock and unlock on their own; lights turn on and off. Some students report that the volume on their radios and televisions has been turned down by unseen hands. Maybe the resident ghost of Roberta believes the music or shows are too loud!

Some students believe in the legend so much that they superstitiously make a burn mark on the door of their room to discourage nocturnal visits from Roberta's ghost. This tradition started some time back when a student reported seeing the apparition of a girl enter her room and try to get into bed with her. The startled student attempted to push the spirit away (she touched nothingness) and then saw the ghost dance in circles around her room. Friends suggested she put the burn mark on her door and the ghost never appeared again.

Some residents of Roberta Hall have heard piano music coming from an empty room in the basement. There is no piano in that room. And the sound of music can be heard at odd times bouncing along the hallways—the source unknown.

9

Workman's Chapel

at Northwest Missouri State University

egend has it that this chapel was once totally engulfed in flames, but the structure sustained no damage. The trees and bushes around the church were completely burned, however. One visitor to the church reported that he heard a voice telling him to look under the floorboards for a knife. The man, of course, did not start pulling up floorboards, but rather left the place as quickly as he could. No one knows why there would be a knife under the floor, but some speculate that a priest had at one time committed murder in the sacred place and hidden the knife under the floor.

No evidence was found that a knife has ever been found or a murder committed at this location, but that doesn't make the story any less frightening!

10

Yeater Hall

at Central Missouri State University

H anging about an all-girls dormitory at Central Missouri State University, 50 miles east of Kansas City in Warrensburg, Missouri, is purportedly the ghost of Laura Yeater. When alive, Laura Yeater was the benefactor who painstakingly watched over and cared for the girls staying there. She was the hall's first dorm mother and became well known for her kind and compassionate nature. Is it possible that the spirit of this woman still cares for the girls who reside there?

The numerous stories of ghostly interactions suggest that there is indeed an otherworldly presence in the dormitory. One oft-told story relates that of a girl who was staying alone in the dorm over a break. She mistakenly mixed alcohol and medicine and passed out unconscious on her bed. An emergency 911 call was placed and the girl was saved after rescue personnel broke down her locked door to perform life-saving procedures. After the incident, those involved wondered how the call had been made. The girl did not remember making the call and was most likely unconscious when the call went through. If the door was locked, there was no way for someone else to enter the room and make the call. Was it the spirit of Laura Yeater continuing her duties as housemother?

Some students have reported seeing mysterious lights in the locked upper floors late at night when no authorized personnel would logically be there. One student reports that a security guard noticed lights turned on one night, so he went up to check it out. Unlocking the access door to the floor, he looked around and determined that no one was up there. So he turned the light off and exited the building. As he left Yeater Hall, he turned back around and looked up. The light was back on in the same room of the floor where he had just been! Students speculate that the college will not open up the 3rd floor because of the unexplained happenings there.

One current CMSU student reports that she saw movement in an upper floor window as she passed by on her early morning run. She informed her residence hall administrator who then went to investigate. The administrator later informed the girl that after unlocking the door to that floor, she and a security guard looked all around and found no trace of any living thing. What did the student see, then, on her early morning jog? She believes it was the spirit of Laura Yeater looking out over her charges, ensuring their well-being from beyond the grave.

11

Herr House

Eerie activity reported in and around Herr House at Park University, just north of Kansas City in Parkville, Missouri, suggests that this place is haunted.

S tudents at the college relate tales of seeing the apparitions of two women dressed in early 1900s clothing floating along one of the hallways. Other students have heard bizarre sounds coming from the back of the building as they pass by. The sounds are muffled and definitely creepy. Legend has it that two unfortunate young women hung themselves in the closet of one of the rooms within the structure. Whether this legend is true or not remains to be proven. The exact room in which the supposed event took place is not known, but supposedly, the room is still used and only the closet blocked off.

12

Jenkin and Barbara David Theater

at Park University

T he Jenkin and Barbara David Theater is believed to be haunted by the ghost of its namesakes. Students have reported seeing the apparition of a man wearing a gray suit, said to be Mr. David. Others report seeing the vision of a woman moving her arms about as if gesturing during a play.

Barbara and Jenkin David both had considerable backgrounds in theater. Mr. David was a professor at Park College for many years. He and his wife established the Bell Road Barn Playhouse—a forum that provided students and the Parkville community with acting experience and even academic credit. Does this thespian couple continue to watch over budding actors and actresses on the campus of Park University today?

13

The Old Jackson County Jail

The small space that I entered felt dark and oppressive and more than a little spooky. It is referred to as cell number 1, and even though I did not feel nauseous, as some visitors report when they enter, I could tell this place was not just another old building.

The Jackson County Jail, at 200 South Main Street in Independence Square, was built in 1859 with the Marshal's house alongside it. Made of limestone blocks with iron doors, it had twelve cells--six downstairs and six upstairs. During the time of construction, tensions were extremely high between citizens in the area. The town, state, and country were divided over whether to abolish slavery. Just a few years prior, the Kansas territory had been opened for settlement, but the issue of slavery was left up to popular rule. This caused much violence and unrest as many on both sides of the problem fought to make Kansas their own.

In 1862, although the Confederates had won major battles and Missouri's governor and legislators had all voted to secede, the state of Missouri was held in the Union by military force. Local fighting was in abundance and guerilla fighters, such as Quantrill's Raiders, were right at the heart of it all.

Then it was decreed by Order Number 10 that any person (man, woman, or child) aiding a band of guerillas would be jailed. Soon, the Jackson County Jail was overflowing with

The Old Jackson County Jail and Marshal's Home in Independence, Missouri, was built in 1859.

women and children--sometimes 20 persons to a cell. When they could fit no more, other buildings in the area were used to house more 'criminals'. One delapidated building collapsed, causing the deaths of five women and injuring others. Included amongst the casualties were relatives of outlaws "Bloody" Bill Anderson and the Younger brothers.

The old jailhouse saw many deaths in its day. Deputy Marshal Henry Buggler was killed while on guard duty during an attempted jail break in 1866. He was fighting off armed gunmen as they tried to enter the jail and was shot to death in the master bedroom upstairs. Marshal Jim Knowles, who lived in the adjoining Marshal's home, lost his life trying to settle a fight between two prisoners during the Civil War time period.

The 1859 jail is reported to be haunted by a number of spirits. The old structure saw deaths by individuals on both sides of the law.

Perhaps most unsettling of all is the knowledge that several hangings occurred within the jailhouse itself. Prisoners were tied up and strung over the second floor balcony.

Frank James spent nearly six months in the jail. In 1882, famous outlaw Jesse James was killed and fearing a similar fate, his brother Frank began negotiating his surrender with the governor of Missouri. During those negotiations, Frank James occupied a cell in the Jackson County Jail.

By 1901, another section had been added to the back of the jail to house chain gangs. Finally in 1933, the building was decommissioned as a jail. It found further use for regional relief services (WPA—Works Progress Administration) during the depression years. In its more than 70 years as a working jail, the structure housed all kinds of occupants and saw multiple deaths. Are the spirits of any of them still around today, unable to shake their attachment to the place?

When visiting the old Jackson County Jail, the most notable place for supernatural phenomenon is in cell number 1 (on the right as you enter). Many visitors report feeling sick to their stomach, light-headed, and just generally creepy—like something otherworldly is sharing the same space with them. There were two cold spots in the cell that I felt as I walked around, and I definitely felt like I was not the only person (or soul) in the room. At one point, I actually looked over my shoulder behind me to see who else had entered. Of course, no one had—at least no one that I could see.

It is said that ghosts of the women and children who were jailed here haunt the place. Witnesses have described the sounds of children and have seen child-like apparitions. Others have reported seeing the visage of a cat, most often in the residential portions of the building. GhostVigil.com reported that some visitors to the jail have smelled a strong tobacco or cigar scent as they wandered about the place. The smell passed by them as if on a breeze--strong for an instant, then slowly faded away.

On my self-guided tour, I heard footsteps moving heavily down the center hallway between the cells. I was the first in my party to enter so I know it was not anyone that came with me! I did not see the apparition of a man in a blue uniform, but there are reports stating that others have seen this ghost standing in the middle of one of the cells on the lower level. Could it be one of the soldiers held here during those turbulent times before, after, and during the Civil War? Or is it possibly the specter of Marshal Jim Knowles or even Henry Buggler, both of whom were killed here?

So many happenings in such a relatively small space are quite remarkable. Considering the violent times in which this jail existed, however, it is not surprising that the place has paranormal activity. Could the strange occurrences be caused by the spirits of women and children, officials working at the place, or prisoners that drew their last breath in the limestone enclosure? We may never know.

14

Tryst Falls

A few miles east of Kearney, Missouri, on Highway 92, is a beautiful waterfall called Tryst Falls. It is a picturesque site with picnic and playground areas that make it the perfect spot for families or couples looking for some peace and quiet.

Tryst Falls was Clay County's first park and is located along Williams Creek. The land was first owned by a family who operated a

Beautiful Tryst Falls is rumored to have a haunted past.

The picnic area nestles next to Tryst Falls. A children's playground is just beyond the trees.

mill in the 1840s and 1850s. County historian, Mrs. Robert Steele Withers, believed the park was once a lover's meeting place and picnic site for those looking for something of a 'tryst.' But beware--the beautiful location belies a scary legend.

Late at night, amidst the soothing sound of water rushing over a large stone precipice, locals have seen a woman standing—poised precariously on the lip of the falls. Some say she is holding a bundle, others believe she is getting ready to jump over the edge. Legend states that she was a slave woman who brought her baby there to escape their life of servitude. Her baby can be heard crying and the sound echoes hauntingly off the rocks of the falls and all around the little valley that encloses it.

15

The Visitor

Myrtle and her husband Alan liked to have fun--sometimes too much. But what happened to them in the dead of night in their very home made them believe there were other forces at work in the world besides what they could see in flesh and blood. Here's Myrtle's story:

Her leg was being pulled—literally. "Quit doing that Alan!" she grumbled. Myrtle was sleepy and not in the mood for games. But the grip on her ankle only tightened. She sat up to tell him off and then realized her husband was lying next to her on the bed—not on the floor near where her leg had been dangling.

Panicking, she screamed "Let me go!" and tried to jerk her leg free. It was dark in the bedroom, but she could not see anyone beside her. Her struggles woke her husband up and they both searched for the source of the violence—but could see nothing.

Despite the lack of a visible physical presence, however, Myrtle's ankle was held in a vice-like grip and being pulled strongly. It seemed the intent was to pull Myrtle off of the bed—but for what reason?

By now, the couple was totally freaked out. There was not a person anywhere near the bed. But Myrtle was definitely being pulled by a strong force. For some reason, they both knew instinctively that they could not let her fall out of bed or something horrifying would happen. Myrtle desperately began clutching at the bed sheets, scrambling to stay on the bed. Alan had one hand under her arm and one hand holding the bedpost behind their heads pulling away from the evil force with all his might.

They could feel the hatred emanating from the side and foot of the bed and it seemed to be directed towards Myrtle. Finally, together, they somehow pulled Myrtle's leg free from its evil clasp and huddled on the bed together for a few minutes. No sounds could be heard in their darkened home except for their own heavy breathing.

Alan got up and turned the lights on and inspected the entire house. No one was in the house or appeared to have been in the house with them. Their front and back doors were still locked (as they had been when they had gone to bed). They did not sleep the remainder of the night.

The Kinnemans continued to live in that house for many years afterward, but never experienced any additional paranormal activity. They believe the evil spirit was a very strong warning telling them to follow a more straight and narrow path. The experience made such an impression that they took the message to heart and changed their lives from that point forward.

"Do I believe in ghosts?

No, but I'm afraid of them."

—Marquise du Deffand

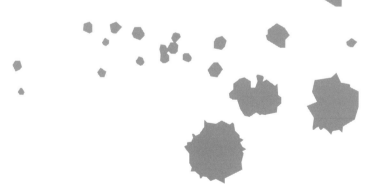

16

The Majestic Steakhouse

Fitzpatrick's Saloon, a three story bar and bordello, opened its doors in downtown Kansas City, Missouri in 1911. Through the years, the structure has provided a variety of goods and services to the public. It has housed a haberdashery (men's clothing store), a speakeasy during the Prohibition time period, and a place of ill-repute. The establishment was also used as a prominent meeting place for Kansas City's 'political boss' Tom Pendergast and other city leaders early in the century.

The Majestic Steakhouse, featuring juicy steaks, smooth jazz, and great cigars, now resides in the purportedly haunted Old Fitzpatrick Building in downtown Kansas City, Missouri.

Today, the Old Fitzpatrick Building houses the Majestic Steakhouse. The restaurant hosts live jazz music in the basement and a cigar club upstairs, but good food and music are not the only attractions for this Kansas City landmark. This historic place houses several ghosts as well--if all the reports are true.

Apparitions of several different women have been seen over the years at The Majestic Steakhouse, mainly on the stairs leading down to the live jazz area and on the second floor. The head chef told X Magazine that several times he saw a woman wearing a red dress with tassels hanging from it. She never responded to his inquiries about whether she needed assistance, solidifying the thought that it was a specter and not a real person.

Could it be possible that this lavishly dressed apparition is one of the 'ladies of the night' who worked at the original brothel? Or is she possibly a patron of the speakeasy from the Roaring 20s?

Visitors have reported seeing the ghostly image of a man dressed in a 1920s/30s style double breasted suit sitting at the bar. His hat sits on the bar next to him. He may have been there to meet with the head of Kansas City's political machine—Tom Pendergast. Pendergast's strong-handed methods were often questioned.

It is thought this person's meeting may have ended badly.

Harry S. Truman got his start in politics with backing by the Pendergast machine. During the Pendergast era (roughly 1890-1940), Kansas City saw much beneficial growth and development. Many boulevards and parks were developed including the Country Club Plaza--but that growth also came with a price. Much of the construction work done during this time was done by the Pendergast Readi-Mix Concrete Company, and the period was full of violence and corruption.

The ban on alcohol was virtually meaningless in Kansas City, even though statewide prohibition was passed in neighboring Kansas in 1881. Thirsty citizens near the Missouri border simply crossed over the state line and headed to Kansas City's Main Street. Indeed, Missouri never passed a state-issued ban on alcohol and the environment within the city was such that even when federal prohibition was passed in 1919, it really did not affect Kansas City all that much. Pendergast's control within the civic arena was such that no arrests were ever made by Kansas City's federal prosecutor for illegal alcohol use.

The speakeasy influence within the Old Fitzgerald building itself may provide the reason regulars have also seen the apparition of various ladies down in the jazz room--where the speakeasy existed for so many years. These spirits appear to be dressed for a night out and exude a feeling of happiness and pleasure.

Who haunts this historic landmark? Could it be a flapper from the Roaring '20s, a lady of ill-repute, or a businessman whose meeting ended poorly?

The Kansas City Ghost Hunters reported to X Magazine that when they toured the place, they felt the presence of a spirit bartender, a ghost in the jazz room, and the eerie presence of a woman who was murdered on the second floor in the 1930s.

Patrons and workers have reported hearing slamming doors and footsteps on the stairs between the restaurant and the jazz area in the basement. They also report the door knobs on locked doors jiggling as if someone was trying to get in, but when they investigated, no one was there.

Hidden beneath the grandeur of the Majestic's historical place in Kansas City lore are stories upon stories of political intrigue, underground activities, and fancy ladies. Oftentimes it was a rough and tumble world where all was not as it seemed. So who haunts this splendid place today? Most likely a mishmash of characters from a shady past!

17

The Summer White House

President Harry S. Truman's home in Independence, Missouri

The tour guide stood at the front gate of the beautifully preserved home. Tall and proud, he seemed to be standing guard over the historic site rather than simply waiting to conduct his next tour of the Truman Home in Independence, Missouri. I spoke to him about his experiences working at the historic home, and I could hear the deep respect he had for the Truman family and the place they held in both United States and Kansas City history. My tour guide said that although he had never seen any sort of ghostly activity himself, he had heard stories from both colleagues and visitors.

The white, two-story home is steeped in memories of the past. "If only these walls could talk," I thought as I visited with the park ranger. Our conversation revealed that many interesting things had occurred in the house.

President Truman had held a radio broadcast from this very location the night before the 1948 presidential election. In this home the president was informed that North Korea had invaded their neighbor to the South. But is it only these snapshots from the past that linger around the place? Or does the spirit of America's 33rd President still enjoy his peaceful home from beyond the grave?

Both employees and touring visitors have reported seeing the ghost of Harry S. Truman relaxing in his living room surrounded by his phonograph record collection and family photographs. Others have reported that the odor of his favorite bourbon can be smelled in that very same relaxing location.

Some people have reported getting unexplainable whiffs of men's cologne as they pass by the stairs leading to the second floor. It should be noted that Mrs. Truman left all of her husband's belongings to sit just as they appeared before he passed away. All of his toiletry items were left alone. In fact, if you were to walk into the room, it would look exactly as it did on the day he died.

That could explain some of the ghostly ambiance that lingers about the place. Indeed, very few people outside the family can view the private quarters upstairs, but those who have seen it say it is like stepping back in time. Even those not given to believing in ghosts can easily imagine that President or Mrs. Truman could simply step around the corner at any minute.

Some visitors have reported hearing movement in the private areas of the house, even though no one else was in attendance. One visitor heard piano music coming from the music room just moments after she and the guide had exited it! President Truman's daughter, Margaret, was a celebrated singer and indeed the whole family thoroughly enjoyed music.

Could these unexplainable incidents point to a spiritual presence? Does Harry remain in the house playing the piano

Does President Truman's spirit linger about "The Summer White House?"

and relaxing in his nearly lifelong home? The tour guide firmly believes that if there are ghosts from the Truman family still roaming about the place, they are kind and generous spirits-- pleased that their home has been so well cared for.

Except for their time spent in Washington, D.C., 219 North Delaware Street in Independence was the primary residence for Harry and Bess Truman for the majority of their lives. They lived together in this house from the time they were married in June, 1919 to when they both passed away. The home has also been referred to as "Wallace House" because it actually belonged to Bess's mother, Madge Wallace. Bess had been living there with her mother since her father's death some time earlier. At the beginning of their marriage, Harry was putting a lot of money and energy into his haberdashery (men's clothing store) in downtown Kansas City, so staying with family made sense financially.

By 1922, the haberdashery had failed and Harry and Bess could not afford to live elsewhere, so they continued living in the family home in Independence. That same year, Harry entered the political arena as a Jackson County judge. He was backed by Kansas City's shady political boss Tom Pendergast. Although the Pendergast machine was known for their strong-handed methods, Truman was somehow able to maintain his integrity and independence. He was smart enough to know that in order for him to be able to help the citizens of Jackson County, he had to be able to work with Pendergast—not against him.

Truman went on to the Senate in 1935 and then the vice presidency under Roosevelt in 1944. In 1945, Truman returned to Independence to attend the funeral of Tom Pendergast. Although he received a lot of negative attention for his appearance (Pendergast had been in jail for tax evasion), Truman contended that Pendergast had been a friend and attending the funeral was the right thing to do.

When President Franklin D. Roosevelt died in April of 1945, Truman took the presidential oath. For the better part of the next decade, President Truman faced many challenges. Helping to end World War II and dropping the atomic bomb on Japan are two major challenges for which Truman is well known.

During his presidency, Truman was rarely able to go home to Independence, but he made as many trips as his duties allowed. Many Christmases were spent there along with summer vacations.

The Truman House, built in 1867 by Bess Truman's grandfather, George Gates, is managed by the National Park Service.

In fact, during his presidency, the home in Independence became known as "The Summer White House."

After leaving politics in January 1953, Truman retired to Independence and lived there with Bess until his death on December 26, 1972. He was 88 years old. Mrs. Truman continued to live in the 14-room Victorian home that her grandfather had built around 1867. Upon her death in 1982, Mrs. Truman willed most of her possessions within the house to the people of the United States. As a National Historic Site, the Park Service staff care for the home, its furnishings, and the personal possessions of Harry S. Truman and Bess Wallace Truman. Visitors can see library books, clothing, and even Harry's last automobile. Many other personal items were donated to the Harry S. Truman Presidential Library and Museum—a place dedicated to preserving the papers, books, and other historical materials relating to Truman. It was a project that was very dear to Harry's heart and he dedicated many hours in his retirement organizing its contents and readying them for the public.

Throughout their lives, the Trumans were involved within the Independence community. Harry's first job was at a soda fountain (now Clinton's Soda Fountain and Gifts) just down the road in historic Independence Square. Later in life, the former President regularly took early morning walks down the tree-lined streets visiting with friends and neighbors along the way. Before, during, and after his presidency, Harry Truman was a very friendly and accessible man. He would often find admirers waiting to speak with him at his front gate when he returned home. Harry was always accommodating with a kind word and an autograph if asked. He once said that if people were ever to stop appearing at his gate, he would most surely miss them.

The nice quiet neighborhood where they called home was the very picture of hometown charm. In fact, the area around the Truman Home has been designated as the Harry S. Truman Historic District and is also a National Historic Landmark. The preserved site includes the two adjacent homes where Mrs. Truman's brothers and their families lived. Across the street is the home where President Truman's aunt and cousins lived. It is easy to imagine that the area looks very much the same today as it did when the Trumans lived there.

Harry S. Truman was a down-to-earth man with Middle American ideals and ethics. He enjoyed a simple life in this house before and after his presidency. Does his ghostly spirit enjoy this peaceful home still?

Quotes I like from Harry S. Truman include:

"I never gave anybody hell. I just told the truth and they thought it was hell."

"The only thing new in this world is the history that you don't know."

"The buck stops here."

Although President Truman didn't originate the phrase, he did adopt it and make it famous. Displayed prominently on his desk in the White House was a sign containing those words. The other side of the sign read "I'm from Missouri."

18

a beloved pet

Pets are often our friends, companions, and confidantes. They mean so much to us because these loyal animals never let us down and are always there for us when we need them. But is it possible for our furry friends to continue this closeness with us even after they are gone? Many believe wholeheartedly that they can and do. Kathy Cox is one such supporter of this comforting idea and believes that the spirit of her poodle, Nikki, has remained in her home and by her side even after his passing.

The little poodle joined the family as a puppy. His tight, rust-colored curls were too adorable to ignore and soon everyone in the family was eating out of his paw. When someone would sit on the couch, Nikki would try his hardest to jump up with them or simply curl up next to their feet on the floor. He often cracked the family up with his funny quirks; he hated hard floors and if forced to walk through the kitchen, would skitter and prance like he was walking on hot coals. At night, the poodle would join Kathy in bed. After tiptoeing around in a circle, as if trying to find the exact right time and location to lie down, Nikki usually kept Kathy's head warm as he made himself comfortable as a nightcap. Since Kathy had a waterbed, his movements were quite pronounced when he performed this nightly routine.

Nikki had a long life, and after his death his spirit seemed to fill the house in Liberty. One night, as Kathy lie in bed just before sleep overtook her, she felt tiny little footsteps next to her.

She was on her side and could feel the bed dipping down along the length of her back as if little feet (or paws) were walking on the bed. The sensation was so real that Kathy reached her hand back to feel what was causing the movement. But nothing was there. Quite unsettled, she turned the light on to double-check. Nothing. Reflecting on the incident, Kathy was sure it was the spirit of Nikki coming to join her for a good night's sleep. The little ghostly paws mimicked the dancing circle her poodle always did prior to lying down.

This instance was not the only time Kathy experienced the ghost of her beloved pet. At times while sitting on the couch, Kathy could feel warmth around her feet and legs as if Nikki's spirit was curling up next to her on the floor. She would also feel the presence of the poodle next to her on the couch as she watched television. Sometimes the feeling was so strong that she would forget Nikki was gone and absentmindedly reach out to pet him—but her hand would only touch air.

Many people treat their pets like members of the family. Pets can fill up such a big part of our lives that when they die we feel a huge sense of loss. It comes as no surprise then, to learn of stories about ghost cats and dogs remaining with their human families even after they are gone—providing a marvelous sense of comfort to their human friends.

19

A Tale of Murder and Injustice

Some thirty years ago, a young woman was last seen driving her car towards home from her parents' house. It was late on a Wednesday night. The dirt roads leading the back way home from Highway 92 were lit only by the moonlight. No streetlights helped guide her path.

The girl was missing for two weeks before her body was found in a clearing well off the dirt road. She had been abused and murdered and left to decay in the woods behind an old barn in the vast farmland 20 miles north of Kansas City, Missouri. Her car was found abandoned five miles down the road from where the body was discovered.

The police questioned the victim's husband, family, neighbors, coworkers, and others that might have had information that could have been helpful. Citizens in the area were scared to death--afraid that a killer was running free in the area. Murder in this rural community was not common in the least. One passerby that night reported that they had seen a young woman by her car on the lonely road, but they did not stop and no one saw the girl alive again.

It is believed that her car had broken down and since this was well before the convenience and safety that cell phones provide, she was forced to walk to find assistance. It is estimated that someone picked her up under the guise of helping her, but with, in fact, the intent to do her harm.

Something terrible happened behind this abandoned barn near Highway 92. Does a restless spirit haunt the area now?

Are the sad, eerie sounds heard late at night those of a young girl's spirit crying out for justice?

The killer must have known the area in order to know just the right place where the horrible deeds and disposal of the body could be carried out without witness.

Just after this tragedy, a mother and daughter were followed home from a nearby hospital where they were visiting a sick relative. They were murdered. Their killer was apprehended, and while people thought the deaths may have been related, no proof of any connection was found. The young woman's roadside murder is still unsolved.

It is said that sometimes in the dead of night, shrieks can be heard coming from behind the abandoned barn in the clearing where the young lady was murdered and her body left to nature. The sound sends chills up the spine. Other times, it is a sad lonely wail that is heard, possibly the innocent young woman's spirit plaintively searching for her killer and some peace at last.

20

A Voice in the Dark

a rural cemetery north of Kansas City

F riends Ruth and Dawn were nervous. And not just a little bit. What had started out as a passing comment made in jest soon found them in the middle of this tiny cemetery on a pitch-black night in the middle of December. There was

The raspy voice of a spirit was digitally recorded by two teens one night in this graveyard. "Just go away!" it said.

snow on the ground from the last storm, and the girls were bundled up. They felt ready for whatever they might find and were armed with a digital camera and a tape recorder for their first and only ghost hunting experience.

The previous weekend, they had been watching a ghost hunting show on television and decided to try it out themselves. Ruth had received a digital camera as an early Christmas present, and Dawn had found a digital tape recorder in her family's hall closet.

Loaded down with their 'tools,' they parked at the entrance to the cemetery and entered cautiously. They felt a little foolish at first and just sort of wandered carefully around—respectful of where they stepped amongst the graves. Soon, however, they were caught up in reading some of the headstones and sort of relaxed into the experience. They spread a blanket down on a bare patch beneath one of the winter-bare trees and settled upon it to get their bearings. They decided that the first thing they would do was try to capture proof of spirits via the digital camera. Ruth took it out of her bag and began taking pictures.

View of the rural cemetery the girls may have seen that night, sloping gently into pastures.

She pointed it at specific gravesites, at the tree above them, out toward the horizon, and down the hill away from the cemetery. As she pointed it at Dawn to see if any spirits were hanging around her as well, she chuckled a little. Dawn would totally freak out if they found a ghoul hovering over her later! Ruth sat back down and the teens began to view the photos just taken. They laughed nervously as the light from the view screen flickered eerily in the night. Television shows had educated them on what to look for—bright round lights (called orbs) or a series of orbs strung together. Excitedly, they viewed the photos, but did not see anything strange. No lights, no orbs, no visual clues that there were ghosts there with them in the graveyard that night.

Disappointed, but not deterred, the girls set up the tape recorder on the blanket next to them. They made sure that nothing around them would make any sound (like their winter coats or their shoes) and started recording. Dawn spoke quietly into the nothingness. "Hi, I'm Dawn, and this is Ruth. We are wondering if there is anyone here that would like to talk with us." It was an invitation to the spirits--a way to let them know that they were willing to listen.

No immediate response was heard, and the girls looked at one another and shrugged. It was probably too much to ask for a ghost to just pop out and say "Hi." A car drove past along the highway on the other side of the cemetery, and other than a brisk breeze moving through the tree above them, the night was quiet again. A few seconds passed, a dog barked and was answered by another and still another, like a little doggie phone chain. The newbie ghost hunters sat still for quite a while longer and when no other sounds came out of the eerie dark night, Dawn turned off the tape recorder and prepared to replay it.

"Are you ready?" asked Dawn. Ruth nodded and took a deep breath. Dawn pushed the play button, and they heard Dawn's tentative introduction: "Hi, I'm Dawn, and this is Ruth. We are wondering if there is anyone here that would like to talk with us." Then there was silence, then the car, then silence, then the canine communication network. A few more seconds of silence, and then they heard a scratchy voice that could have been a woman's. "Just away." Both girls froze. What? "Just away?" What does that mean? But before they could speak, the same voice was heard on the recording—this time more clearly and forcefully:

This rural cemetery, north of Kansas City, is reportedly haunted.

"Just go away! I'm tired!"

The girls looked around almost frantically. Was the voice's owner talking to *them*? And who was it? They did not stay to ponder those questions at the cemetery. The friends grabbed all of their belongings and raced for their car. Over the next few weeks and months, they would pass by the place often, but they never returned at night. And they never forgot their ghostly encounter.

"Just go away! I'm tired!"

21

Reed Cemetery

The Reed cemetery in Clinton County, Missouri, is an old family graveyard. The area in which it lies is still quite rural, and it is easy to picture a family farm nearby, its occupants worrying about the crops or the livestock. Looking at the old inscriptions surrounded by the beautiful country atmosphere

Reed Cemetery may be haunted by Civil War-era spirits. This gravestone marks the mother of two sons who were lost in the war.

reminds any observer that today's modern life is not the only one filled with stress. But are the spirits of those buried there still worrying about their struggles from beyond the grave? The answer may be "yes." Residents of the area report seeing lights flickering at night within the area of the oldest grave sites. When investigated, nothing out of the ordinary is found.

In the oldest part of the cemetery, I found gravestones dating prior to the Civil War. Two headstones show that both sons from the same family were lost in the war within the same year. Is it possible the spirits of those boys returned home from the tragedies of war to their beloved Missouri farm? Do they linger still?

"And in the end,

it's not the years in your life that count.

It's the life in your years."

—Abraham Lincoln

22

The Guardian

Another old cemetery nearby offers more than a walk through history. It reportedly also offers a brush with a graveyard guardian.

Siblings Lane and Angela told me a story about how one summer evening they were out searching for their dog Scout who had run away from the farm. Being out in the country, the little terrier was not confined to a fence and had free reign of the area. The dog was aptly named--every morning she left to scout the area for interesting things to do and smell, but was always back in time for supper. This time, she had been gone for two days, and the kids were worried. After supper, they searched the fields surrounding their house and were calling out her name. It was getting dark as they neared the old cemetery that adjoined their land when they heard a sort of rustling in that general direction. Thinking that Scout had possibly gotten herself stuck in the fence that surrounded the graveyard, they approached to see what was making the sound. As they got closer, they could tell that it was, in fact, an animal moving about in the brush around the cemetery. But it was not stuck in the rusted iron fence, and it was definitely not their dog Scout!

It was a huge black dog, and it made not a sound--not a growl or a whimper or even a bark. It just slowly rose to its feet as it spied the youths and began to trot at an angle away from them. Spooked a little by the odd behavior, the kids turned to go home when they noticed that the hound was not actually leaving the area—it was moving around the edge of the cemetery and coming back to where they were. It was circling them!

Chills shot through them and they froze. The canine turned to face directly toward them, and they could clearly see its eyes were shining red in the moonlight. At that point, Angela and Lane could not run fast enough away from the cemetery. They sprinted back through the fields, over a final hill and into their own backyard. What they had seen was not a normal dog and they would never forget its eerie presence in the graveyard that night.

Had it been a 'devil dog' or 'hellhound' that Lane and Angela had seen? Such supernatural creatures have appeared all through ancient mythology, serving mainly as guards to the underworld. Legend and folklore sometimes feature these mythological canines as harbingers of death or as guardians of portals to the world of the dead. In Britain, folklore has it that the 'Black Dog' is a ghostlike being that, while generally considered wicked, has been known to act in a kindly manner.

While the darker side of these stories is frightening, people in some cultures feel comforted at the appearance of such an animal. They believe that seeing such a creature at a loved one's grave is an assurance that the deceased will be watched over and their spirit safely guarded from harm.

23

The Musical Ghost

Karen was out for her early morning walk. The sun was just beginning to creep over the horizon, and the cool air felt good. She could tell that this July day, just beginning, was going to be a hot one. Karen and her family had recently moved to a newly built subdivision about 30 miles south of Kansas City. The small town was growing dramatically, and Karen loved the area. The only drawback was that their new neighborhood had some very old residents—from a cemetery just around the block.

It was a garden-type cemetery that was well-kept and beautifully manicured. So other than the mental aspect of dead people being buried close by, there was really nothing about which to complain. In fact, the peaceful place had become the halfway point in her exercise routine. She would walk to the cemetery, turn around, and then head back home.

When Karen had started out toward the cemetery that morning, it seemed just like all the previous mornings before it. But as she would soon discover, there was nothing remotely normal or routine about her walk that morning. As she approached her turning around spot under the big tree just inside the graveyard, she heard music. It was some sort of violin music. "That's odd," she thought. "It is just now getting light, why would someone be practicing so early?" Something about the beautiful notes drew her further into the cemetery. Instead of heading back toward her home, Karen's feet seemed to move of their own accord toward the music. As she walked, the notes grew louder, though remained soft and whispery in nature. Suddenly, the music stopped. Karen halted her progress and looked

Does a ghostly musician play her violin in a graveyard like this one?

around her as if coming out of a trance. She found herself in the middle of the cemetery. Directly in front of her was a grave that looked very old. The headstone was not smooth and the edges of it were rough and worn by the elements. Through the gray early morning light, Karen saw that the tombstone was simply inscribed "Julia Ann" and below that was a picture of a violin carved beautifully into the old stone!

24

Gravity Hill

There are many places around the world that have a phenomenon known as Gravity Hill. Kansas City's Gravity Hill is located south of the city in a rural spot of Cass County, where Mo-D meets East 299th St., at the railroad tracks near Cleveland, Missouri.

As you drive along the road, you can see beautiful countryside scenery all around you. If you park your car pointing uphill, put it in neutral and take off the brake, the car actually moves forward instead of backward as you would expect it to. The sensation is quite odd--it feels like you are either being pushed by some unseen force or being pulled by one! It's called Gravity Hill because it appears to defy gravity!

So how does this happen?

One story in Kansas City lore says that a man died at this spot after his car slid off the icy road. Now he helps others by pushing apparently stalled cars up the hill. (I mean, you are stopped in the middle of the road. It makes sense that a ghost would think you were having car trouble!)

Some people call it a magnetic hill and believe there is a sort of warp in the Earth's gravity. Doubters of the supernatural explanation (ok, scientists) say the entire experience is simply an optical illusion. The lay of the land and position of the trees make it appear that you are on an uphill slope when actually, you are not. The view of the horizon is usually limited, so the naked eye cannot judge whether the car is pointing up or down.

Is Gravity Hill a myth, a scientific oddity, or an optical illusion? It is up to you to decide. Could there be a ghost with a good heart (and strong back!) helping out those of us who appear to need it? We could pack up our levels and hike out there to investigate. But I think we should enjoy the strangeness of the experience and imagine a benevolent spirit helping out those in need.

"Ghosts only exist for those who wish to see them."

—Holtei

25

The Odd Fellows Home

Why is it that things shrouded in darkness and mystery draw us like moths to the flame? I think it is because without all the facts, our imaginations take over. Oftentimes, our brains dream up way more bizarre and frightening details than actual facts ever could. If we are lucky, our forays into the unknown help us find answers that satisfy our curiosity while still thrilling (or scaring) us senseless! That is what ghost hunting is all about—discovering the correct combination of both truth and excitement!

A good example of this phenomenon is the Odd Fellows Home located just south of Liberty, Missouri.

An impressive site from the road, this complex of old brick buildings sits atop the hill like something out of a scary movie. It appears to be looking down on passersby, jealously guarding its secrets from any who may trespass.

But what exactly are those secrets? Several people who visited the site claimed to get a sense of cold spots as they entered especially dark and spooky areas, giving them the impression of a ghostly presence. At one time there were parts of the building that still contained all of the old furnishings from the last residents. Observers to such a scene can't help but wonder if the previous occupants simply grabbed a few things and left—creepy!

Originally on this site was a hotel and health spa called Reed Springs Hotel. It was built in 1888 and was centered around some natural springs that had been found on the property. Similar to those in Excelsior Springs, the three-story high hotel

The Odd Fellows home in Liberty, Missouri, sits eerily at the top of a hill.

catered to the more well-to-do clientele. The large dining room and 108 guest rooms were all lavishly decorated.

The hotel attracted visitors from all over, including one individual that would eventually become grand master of the Odd Fellows—Dr. R. F. Mathews. He visited the hotel for its healing waters, recovered nicely, met and married a girl from Liberty, and settled down in the area to practice medicine. (He later worked at the Odd Fellows home providing care to its residents for many years.)

In 1891, a well-known promoter purchased the hotel and renamed the establishment Winner Hotel, after himself. Soon, however, Mr. Winner's investment was foreclosed upon, and one of America's largest fraternal organizations, the Independent Order of Odd Fellows, purchased the hotel and its surrounding acreage. The Odd Fellows Home was dedicated on May 24, 1895, and the group was soon caring for orphans and aging members of the Order.

In 1900, a fire destroyed the building, but new buildings were immediately constructed and still stand today. In 1951, a 50-bed hospital was added to the complex. The home operated as a rest home, doing much good in the community for many years, until finally closing its doors late in the century. Eventually, it was purchased from the Odd Fellows by a private party.

In 2006, the structure was put on the Most Endangered List by the Missouri Alliance for Historic Preservation. The current owner is very reticent about his plans for the old buildings. Renovations are reported to be underway, but the driveway gates are locked, and the property kept under constant surveillance. This atmosphere of secretiveness that has been created most likely encourages some of the more wild tales and attempts to see what is up on the hill.

The complex also has an air of mystery around it simply because it was owned and operated by the Odd Fellows. The group originated in England as a mutual benefit society— meaning that if a traveling member needed assistance when away from their home, they could call upon another lodge and graciously receive food, lodging, and sometimes even financial assistance. There needed to be a way to identify members, and so the mechanisms for proving membership were created. When the Order came to America, these same traditions came along as well.

The Odd Fellows' meetings are open only to members of the order, which makes some people think they have something to hide or may be covering up something suspicious. In reality, they are only conducting their business affairs—similar to shareholder meetings. The meetings are closed to the public because they are simply a private organization.

There is an initiation ceremony when members join, and although technological advances make them unnecessary, the order uses an antique mechanism for checking membership before their meetings come to order. Some of the urban legends about the Odd Fellows home may be founded in misinformation about its history. And where there is not enough factual information to form a basis, our imaginations come to life.

The Order's motto is: "Amicitia, Amor, et Veritas," meaning "Friendship, Love, and Truth." An instruction given to each new member is inscribed on the official seal: "We command you to visit the sick, relieve the distressed, bury the dead, and educate the orphan." The group does a lot of good around the world and in the communities where they reside.

The more mysterious a place (and the less we know about it), the more ghost stories seem to arise, however. Some people claim to have sneaked into the complex after dark (this author does NOT condone trespassing!) to find bloody handprints on the walls. Other urban legends report the sound of bed springs squeaking, the eerie sounds echoing off the walls and bouncing down empty corridors into nothingness.

So are the legends true? Does the old Odd Fellows Home generate so much thought and discussion about ghostly activity because there really are ghosts of orphans and widows lingering about the place? Or are the stories about the place conjured from overactive imaginations?

The building does strike a remarkable image high atop the hill just off a busy highway. It presents a beautiful visual picture that stirs our minds to all sorts of legend and lore. And what will become of this historic place? The answer remains to be seen.

You want to know whether I believe in ghosts.

Of course I do not believe in them.

If you had known as many of them as I have,

you would not believe in them either.

—Don Marquis

26

The Hotel Savoy

Possible Cause of Death: suicide, accidental death, or
natural causes
Location: bathtub, room 505
Deceased: Betsy Ward

Guests have seen an apparition around the vicinity of room 505 of the Hotel Savoy in downtown Kansas City and believe it to be the ghost of Betsy Ward. The circumstances around this unfortunate death are vague--which leaves many to wonder if her spirit has been unable to find peace and move on. Could the elderly woman's ghost be responsible for the water being turned on by unseen hands in the very same unit where she died? What about the unexplained foot-steps heard outside her room and down the hall? One report even stated that the shower curtain in the bathroom closed by itself.

Built in 1888, the Hotel Savoy is the oldest operating hotel west of the Mississippi River. It hosted many prominent people throughout its days as a stylish stopover for visitors to Kansas City and those traveling on to the West. Theodore Roosevelt and William H. Taft both enjoyed the hotel's beautiful woodwork, rooftop garden and stained glass skylight. Old-time personalities Will Rogers, W.C. Fields and John D. Rockefeller also stayed the night in The Savoy.

In 1903, the hotel added the Savoy Grill--still in operation today as the oldest restaurant in Kansas City. No paranormal activity has been reported at the Savoy Grill, but the murals on the walls make you believe one of the pioneers poised for departure on the Sante Fe Trail could simply step right off the wall and into the room!

After World War II, the hotel fell into disrepair and turned into a flop house. Then for a while it was used as an apartment building.

The old Savoy Hotel has seen many well-known visitors throughout its history. Do any of their spirits remain?

One of the ghosts of the Savoy Hotel is purported to be a man named Fred Lightner, whose gray specter has been spied outside his old apartment. Another person reported hearing music coming from that same apartment when the current resident was not home and later reported that the radio was not on when he returned.

Many decades ago, there were tunnels running under many historic places in Kansas City. Today, most of the tunnels have collapsed, been filled in, or been blocked off for safety reasons. Over the years, there have been accidents and deaths reported in the tunnels under the Savoy--and one particular victim seems to have remained in the vicinity.

The specter of a man has been sighted on several occasions in the basement of the Savoy and is thought to be the cause of unexplained noises and crashes. He appears wearing a purple jacket—no one knows why. It could be a uniform of sorts or simply a fashion statement! The apparition appears as a misty figure, but is clear enough to be described as a man in his 60's with gray hair and a beard.

Some believe there is an increase in ghostly activity whenever there is work being done within the building. Guests and employees have reported seeing the apparition of an unknown woman moving across another guest room. No one knows for sure who

Tunnels running beneath the Savoy Hotel may be home to a ghostly apparition.

she might be for her appearance is very murky and does not show a lot of detail.

Others have reported seeing the ghost of a previous Savoy manager who was killed in a gruesome murder some years back. His visage has been sighted down in the basement, where the terrible deed took place. The man had been working late and an intruder killed him in cold blood.

Can physical activities such as renovations stir up ghosts along with the dust? While workers are pulling out old walls and floorboards to discover interesting artifacts and letters from the past, could they also be reviving ghosts that have been resting for years? Like many old buildings, the Savoy has many secrets we may never know.

The Hotel Savoy was built in 1888.

27

The Muehlebach Hotel

Some ghosts are scary looking. Some just give us the creeps. At the Muehlebach Hotel in downtown Kansas City, their ghost is hauntingly beautiful.

This apparition is referred to in Kansas City lore as the Blue Lady, because she always appears in a blue dress styled similar to those worn in the 1920s. She looks to be around thirty years old and her blonde hair is tucked up neatly into a wide-brimmed hat. The Blue Lady has been seen by guests sitting in a lounge chair in the lobby and moving along the halls. Her visage is so real, that some people have attempted to talk to her. When addressed, the mysterious vision gives no response and seemingly melts away into thin air.

Some believe the Blue Lady is the ghost of an actress who once played at the Gayety Theater next door to the Muehlebach Hotel. The story says she is searching for her lost lover amongst the guests that visit the hotel.

The Hotel Muehlebach opened in 1916 and soon became known for its luxurious atmosphere. Over the years, many famous people stayed there; Harry S. Truman, Elvis Presley, Babe Ruth, and the Beatles are among them. Next door was the Gayety Theater which operated as a theater from 1906 to 1935. It was razed in 1950 to make room for expansions to the Muehlebach.

This prominent landmark has seen many faces appear through their doors to stay the night. Could one of them have decided to stay forever? As far as ghosts go, it wouldn't be too bad to have a quiet, beautiful woman looking over the place from beyond the grave.

A ghost called the Blue Lady is believed to haunt this grand hotel.

The luxurious Hotel Muehlebach opened its doors in 1916.

28

St Mary's Episcopal Church

ating back to 1857, St. Mary's Episcopal Church is one of Kansas City's oldest congregations. The building at 13th and Holmes, downtown, has been the parish's place of worship since 1888. The structure itself is quite impressive with a stunning tower and interesting Gothic arches. Seen from the outside, the stained glass windows give the church a wonderful old-world aura.

As I walked around the beautiful brick building, I could feel a sense of history and a mystical presence surrounding the structure. One particular arched doorway housed a rough wooden door, and it drew my full attention. I felt compelled to reach out and touch the wood and feel its texture. While noted for its special interior features and its striking Gothic architecture, this church is also known for its supposed resident ghost, Reverend Henry David Jardine. Peculiar noises have been heard in various places throughout the church without explanation, and some believe that they are the work of Reverend Jardine.

Reverend Jardine helped to organize the parish and founded two schools during his time as leader of the congregation from 1879 to 1886. He even helped create the hospital that was later to become St. Luke's. But Reverend Jardine had a passionate way about him that created some controversy with certain church members and officials. His mysterious death in St. Louis in 1886 was ruled a suicide, and as a consequence,

Beautiful architecture and stained glass windows help to make St. Mary's Episcopal Church a Kansas City landmark.

An arched wooden doorway hints at things otherworldly.

St. Mary's Church reaches toward heaven. Does the spirit of Reverend Jardine look out from the towers to watch over his congregation?

his body was not buried on consecrated soil. Reverend Jardine was officially exonerated 35 years later, but many believe that his spirit yet remains with his congregation, working hard to clear his good name.

O Death, rock me asleep,

Bring me to quiet rest,

Let pass my weary guiltless ghost

Out of my careful breast."

—Anne Boleyn (1501-1536)

29

The Folly Theater

E arly in the last century (from around 1902 to 1922) Joe Donegan managed to schedule some of the biggest names in showbiz for Kansas City's Folly Theater. History tells us he loved his job. Did he love it so much that he never wanted to quit? Over the years, people in the Folly Theater have reported seeing an apparition of a man wearing a bowler hat--and since Joe

The Folly Theater, in downtown Kansas City, is reported to be haunted.

was rarely seen without his, it is thought that it is probably his ghost that has been spotted.

When the Folly first opened in 1900 (as the Standard Theater), it hosted vaudeville, burlesque, and comedy acts. Within the year, the theater was renamed the Century and changed entertainment direction. Maude Adams, Richard Mansfield, Sarah Bernhardt, Al Jolson, Fannie Brice, Eddie Foy, and the Marx Brothers were some of the famous acts hosted by the theater. Joe Donegan managed the theater and hotel/grill next door and scheduled special events on Saturday evenings after regular theater performances were finished. Prize fights and wrestling were common events, and they brought in the likes of Jack Dempsey, Jack Johnson, and Harry the Great. (Interestingly, Frank James, the outlaw Jesse's brother, was a ticket taker at the theater at one time).

Following the tough depression years, the theater returned to burlesque, but in a new form—striptease. During those years, big names such as Tempest Storm, Ann Corio, and Gypsy Rose Lee graced the stage. From time to time, workers at the theater have reported seeing a ghostly figure of a woman wearing a long flowing gown rushing toward the stage. Could it be an old-time burlesque performer hurrying to hit her cue on stage—her dressing gown covering up her stage costume?

The theater world is famous for its ghosts—almost every one you visit has a resident ghost helping out (or just hanging out). One superstition in many theaters is to leave a light on near the stage after the theater closes up for the night. The story says that this 'ghost light' helps keep the ghost warm and gives them a place to perform. (It also helps in a practical sense so that no one will trip on all of the wires and props lying around—but that is not nearly as much fun to think about!)

Throughout the years, "The Grand Lady of Twelfth Street" was an oasis of laughter and refinement. Now this theater hosts a wide variety of performing artists and other fine arts activities. Does it also host the spirits of some of its past performers? And should it leave a light on for them?

30

The Haunted Asylum

On the eastern loop of Interstate 435 that winds all the way around Kansas City, you will find an area that is a mix of 1950s charm, rural community, and big city activities. The area has Kansas City, Independence, and Raytown addresses all mixed together. If you look up on the hill just past 63rd street, you will spy the remains of one of the scariest places in Kansas City, Missouri.

The location I refer to is now just a clearing with a pile of debris bulldozed over to one side. Many years ago, however, the structure was a psychological health care facility that served the Kansas City area. After years of taking care of the mental health needs of the community, the facility fell into disuse and eventually stood abandoned. It was at this time that ghost hunters (and those just out to scare themselves) from all around the Kansas City Metro area began visiting 'The Raytown Asylum.'

People were drawn to this location because of its history and the fact that it was an abandoned building. However, the stories that returned with just about every visitor were just too frightening and yet ultimately enticing to ignore. As word spread, more and more people attempted to see for themselves what the buzz was all about.

All of the ghostly experiences reported in local lore and legend are simply too numerous to share. It seems that no individual can visit the place without being profoundly affected by its mystical atmosphere. One particular story describes the sound of echoing footsteps and moaning emanating from within the building. The origin is thought to be the spirit of an elderly man who used to be a patient in the old hospital. Is it possible that with his mind crippled with unknown demons, he can not pass on after his death?

Those who study the supernatural have said that there exists enough evidence to prove that spirits who are unable to find peace after death linger to haunt. These sometimes evil, sometimes good spirits seek a continued existence because they have died prematurely and are not willing to abandon the earthly life. Sometimes they are completing an unresolved task in this world.

Stories of the Raytown Asylum describe unexplained phenomenon occurring in the basement or 'bowels' of the structure. One group reports that as they were looking around the boiler room, they all heard something that caused them to take flight. They sprinted out of the basement almost as one. When they reached the main floor, they shared what they had heard—and each account was completely different! The four people heard a siren wailing, a dog barking, a baby crying, and a woman screaming. What could have been the source of the 'noise' to have caused four individuals to hear something so different?

Strangely, many claims to paranormal activity continue at this location even now when the building is gone. Some say they can hear a haunting laugh if they stand on the spot where the asylum used to be. Others report seeing a white, ghost-like apparition float along what appears to be an old sidewalk or pathway that winds around the area.

The following story is a first-hand account by a young man and his group of friends as they ventured to the Raytown asylum on a warm fall night several years ago with the intent to explore its secrets.

An overpowering sense that something definitely was not right had crept upon Lance as he and his friends approached the place, their shoes crunching over the leaves that floated around the old paths on the property. But he forged ahead anyway. This was probably his one and only opportunity to explore the much talked about Raytown Asylum. He wanted to see if all the stories and urban legends were actually true.

Lance and his friends did not enter through the front door of the run-down building, but rather climbed over a crumbling wall into a random room along the side. First impressions upon entering the pitch-black building were dread and eeriness. The room they entered contained showers—sort of like those group showers found in locker rooms at school. Water dripped slowly from a broken pipe in one corner, and the "plop, plop, plop" echoed in the empty space. The sound only seemed to amplify the silence in the rest of the abandoned building. Lance moved through this room and out into the hall. He did not feel the presence of any spirits in that room. He just had a weird feeling in the pit of his stomach—that mixture of dread, anticipation, and excitement. From the 'shower room' the group went down some stairs to what looked like a cellar or basement.

Lance's initial impression was that he was entering a dungeon. The air was damp and moldy even on the warm fall night. Chills went through him at the thought of all the disturbed individuals that might have been there and what might have occurred in the very space he was entering. The beam from his flashlight seemed barely able to penetrate the darkness. Lance stepped through a particularly eerie cold spot in the middle of the stairway as he descended. Was it a draft or something else?

There was not much to see in the basement--other than a deep, deep darkness. But they all heard the piercing shriek (yes, it came from a male) of one friend who explained that he had felt a touch, almost caress along his back—like someone (or the spirit of someone) had walked behind him and trailed their hand from one shoulder blade to the other. After everyone's nervous laughter died down, they really could not get out of the basement fast enough.

After the friends clamored back up to the main level, they searched for a way to get to the upper floors. However, they found metal bars blocking access via what looked like the main stairway. What could be the reason? Who/what was on the upper floors that would require bars? Were authorities trying to keep people from going up, or something from coming down?

These questions intrigued the explorers, and so they searched all the harder for a way up. As Lance looked around, he found that one set of bars on a side stairway had been cut to allow access. So the group carefully filed through to continue their exploration. It was on this next floor that they discovered the most bizarre location any of them had ever seen.

Old hospital beds stood empty (thank goodness!) and aban-doned—their metal frames and dirty mattresses scattered haphazardly throughout the hallways and rooms. There were folding chairs here and there as well as random items such as a huge saw blade—origin unknown. Hospital-type items were everywhere as if the staff had just packed up a few things and left, never to return. Why would a hospital leave behind items that could have been used elsewhere or at least sold for some profit?

Through one of the upper story windows, Lance could see across to a newer building next door. There were people moving about inside that added an eerie edge to the tour. At the time, the group thought the people they saw next door were mental patients that had been moved to a newer building. The thought kind of freaked them out.

(Research note: there is actually a correctional facility next door.)

One of the more disturbing items discovered was a metal filing cabinet full of animal records, like those found at a veterinarian's office. It is unclear how long the building served (if it ever did) as a vet's office. The records spilled on the floor and around the room showed names, type of animal, and other information about various animals. Were these family pets, shelter animals, or research animals? (There is an animal shelter down the road, but how would the two locations have been tied together?) Other documents scattered around on the floor of the room appeared to be death records of animals. Again, questions about what they were referring to put extremely creepy images in everyone's mind.

The tour ended when the group came upon a metal door that was locked and could not be opened. It appeared to be the entrance to an entire other wing. What mysteries of the undead might Lance and his friends have found down that wing? The answer remains unknown because within a year of this late-night adventure, the building was completely destroyed by fire.

Are there spirits still trapped on the grounds of the old mental hospital in Raytown? Are there lost souls that cannot move on for some reason and so remain to haunt the area around where they died? The numerous tales of paranormal activity at this site seem to point most definitely toward "Yes!"

31

Vaile Mansion

I arrived at the Vaile mansion on a beautiful summer day and was getting hot waiting for the front door to be opened. When it was finally cracked open a bit, I could feel a welcome rush of cool air. The face that greeted me, however, was not so welcoming.

I have encountered a few odd looks during the course of my research, but only once did I feel outright animosity directed at me because of one simple question, "Have you ever experienced anything strange while being in this house?"

The curator's face lost all color when I posed my innocent question to her. She backed away, reached for the door, and tried to shut it on me! "We don't appreciate that kind of talk and won't stand for it," was her response, and it honestly took me by surprise. Other than being the standard question I ask everyone in the course of my research, I asked because ever since I was a teenager I had heard that the Vaile Mansion was haunted.

The building has the makings of a proper haunted house. The beautiful Victorian home stands alone in an older part of Independence, Missouri. Its towers reach toward the sky, and the structure's ornately decorated walls provide an extraordinary setting for the tragic story that was rumored to have unfolded within.

Legend states that Mrs. Vaile died of an overdose of morphine in 1883 in one of the upper floor rooms. She had supposedly become completely despondent when her husband, Colonel Vaile, was indicted on charges of fraud. He was a contractor for mail routes leaving Independence and had been charged (along with his partner, L.P. Williamson) with defrauding the government in the course of operating those routes. A second trial that con-

The Vaile Mansion, in Independence, Missouri, is thought to be haunted by its former mistress.

The gorgeous architecture and detailing of the Vaile Mansion make it a must-see in Independence.

cluded after Mrs. Vaile's death found the Colonel innocent of all charges, and he was acquitted. But alas, the happy news came too late for Mrs. Vaile. Legend now purports that she haunts the mansion as an apparition.

Some visitors report feeling a presence in the house that grows stronger as they move along the second floor and near the stairway leading up to the closed off third floor. Many people wonder if Mrs. Vaile's spirit is still in the house and are curious about what happened there.

Trying to get the real story about Mrs. Vaile's death, however, would prove to be harder than I imagined. The pamphlet I received at the mansion contains a conspicuous lack of information about the woman or her life. The document only provides the year she died and states that she was with Colonel Vaile in Europe when they were inspired for the design of the house.

Construction of the 'Crown Jewel of Independence' began in 1880 and was the plan of Colonel Vaile and architect Asa Beebe Cross. After its completion a year later, the Vaile Mansion boasted an advanced gas and water works system along with extensive

The Vaile Mansion is listed on the National Register of Historic Places.

woodwork and paintings on the interior. The home was built with hand-pressed brick and is described as Gothic Victorian.

The combination of the odd lack of information about Mrs. Vaile in the literature I was given and the abnormally strong re-action I received from the curator suggests that there is actually much more to the story than anyone really wishes to share. It is intriguing how such an extreme response can evoke our interest so much more than a simple "No, I've never experienced anything strange!" ever could.

Is the Vaile Mansion haunted? I would really like to know!

32

Union Station

The echoing voices of men, women, and children--some high-pitched, others low, harmonized in an unmistakable murmur, as clear and crisp as a summer's day.

That is what I heard one night as I stood alone in Kansas City's Union Railway Station. The first time I visited Union Station was just after it had been renovated in late 1999. The company I worked for was holding an awards ceremony in one of the new meeting rooms downstairs. It was a Friday night, and I had the place (almost) to myself. I say "almost" because I believe that night there were other souls in the building with me.

There was plenty of time before the meeting started, so I headed up to the main level to look around. The huge long corridor, called the Grand Hall, was totally open, and a visitor could roam just about anywhere. Taking advantage of that fact, I meandered along at my own pace taking in the exhibits around me. Placed here and there were rows of benches positioned along the sides to recreate the waiting room atmosphere, for it was this hall that could hold up to 10,000 people.

Union Station opened its doors in 1914, and was soon filled with travelers. The railway station saw almost 80,000 passengers travel through it in its busiest year thus far, 1917. The year 1921 saw a momentous occasion in that all five Allied commanders from World War I traveled by train into Kansas City's Union Station and met to break ground on the Liberty Memorial--a site dedicated to those who served in WWI and located across the street from the station. In 1945, Union Station saw a record of more than 675,000 passengers (mainly veterans from WWII).

A view of the Grand Hall (or North Waiting Room) of Union Station, where unexplainable voices and other strange sounds have been heard.

However, after that peak in traffic, train travel went into a steady decline as the airline industry grew. Kansas City's Union Station was all but empty for many years until 1996, when a bi-state tax (Missouri and Kansas) was passed for complete renovation of Union Station. On November 10, 1999, Kansas City's Union Station reopened to the public.

It was in the newly reconstructed Grand Hall (the North Waiting Room) that I found myself that night. As I always do when visiting an historical museum or location, I tried to imagine the space as it was many years ago. I sat down on one of the benches to take in the grandeur of the hall and was transported back in time. I closed my eyes and could visualize people busily scurrying back and forth or waiting patiently on the benches for their train to arrive. The space was filled with people dressed in fashions from another era. The women wore hats, and the men wore suits as was the custom when traveling so long ago. I could imagine children running in and around passengers' legs as they chased one another, squealing with delight.

Then I heard something unsettling: The low buzz of thousands of people talking at once; wings flapping (probably pigeons flying around their nests above), children laughing and crying. It was as if someone had turned on the radio right next to my ear--the sounds were so crisp and clear.

A chill ran through me, and I opened my eyes. The scenes I had conjured vanished, but the sounds remained. I stood up and looked around for someone else to share the experience with, but there was not another living soul in that entire space.

I believed (or tried to believe) that the sounds were from a recording of some sort that Union Station was pushing through their sound system to create a realistic ambiance for the exhibits. Being a big fan of the 'total' experience museums should provide visitors, I was extremely impressed. I went to find a co-worker to have them listen as well. But when we returned, there were no sounds in the Grand Hall except our own footsteps on the tiled floors.

To this day, I still have found no confirmation that there were ever any sounds being piped into that waiting area. So what could explain what I heard that night? I remember feeling completely transported back in time—like I was stepping into a painting. At the time, I tried to tell myself it was simply an authentic approach to an historical museum exhibit. Now I feel certain it was something else entirely.

Kansas City's Union Station is reported to be haunted by several spirits.

Many Kansas residents have said over the years that Union Station is haunted. KansasCity.about.com reports tales of unexplainable happenings surrounding Union Station.

Their stories include images of a woman in a black dress walking down the stairs and travelers with luggage wandering about. Not surprising, whistles from nonexistent trains are also heard.

One of the most famous spirits hanging around is said to be Frank Nash, a gangster who was killed during the Union Station Massacre on June 17, 1933.

Places that have seen tragedy are filled with unresolved souls who just cannot seem to move on to a peaceful place. Could the sounds I heard that night in the deserted Union Station have been a replay of events just prior to the Union Station massacre? What exactly happened that day?

It was summer, 1933. The country was captivated with gangsters and their lifestyles—looking at their daring exploits as sensational thrills. However, the incident that occurred outside Kansas City's Union Station that day shocked Americans into realizing just how violent these criminals and their misdeeds were becoming.

The Union Station Massacre occurred while several law enforcement officers were returning Frank Nash to the U.S. Federal Penitentiary in Leavenworth, Kansas. He had escaped the prison and had been on the run since October 19, 1930. On June 16, the day before the murders, two FBI agents and a police chief from Oklahoma apprehended Nash in Hot Springs, Arkansas. From there, they took him to Fort Smith, Arkansas and boarded the Missouri Pacific train to Kansas City's Union Railway Station.

When the train arrived at Kansas City's Union Railway Station the next morning (June 17, 1933) the group was met by two additional FBI agents and two Kansas City Police officers. All seven peace officers escorted the handcuffed Nash from the train, through the lobby of the KC Union Station, and out to the Chevrolet they had parked directly in front of the east entrance to the Station. It was there that friends of the fugitive Frank Nash were waiting to ambush them all and free their compatriot.

The gunmen were later identified as Charles Arthur "Pretty Boy" Floyd, Vernon Miller, and Adam Richetti. Nash and three officers were already in the car when two men charged from behind a green Plymouth parked a mere six feet away. Both attackers were armed, and one had a machine gun. One of them yelled "Let 'em have it!" and at that point, another man crouched behind a nearby parked car started shooting. Two officers standing just next to their car,

A plaque was placed in remembrance of the law enforcement agents who died in the line of duty at Union Station on June 17, 1933.

Hermanson and Grooms, were shot and killed immediately. FBI Agent Caffrey on the other side of the car was shot in the head before he could climb into the driver's seat.

Chief Reed, one of the original captors of Nash, had also been shot and killed as he sat next to his prisoner. The final victim that day was Frank Nash--shot as he sat in the car awaiting his return to prison.

The gunman raced up to the car, looking for Nash inside. A witness heard one of them shout "They're all dead. Let's get out of here!" As they were running back to their car, a KC Police Officer came from Union Station and started firing at them. It is thought that he hit "Pretty Boy" Floyd, but it didn't stop him, and all of the gunmen got to their car and sped away. Survivors reported that the entire episode lasted less than 30 seconds.

The rescue attempt had failed. The outlaws had killed four officers of the law and Frank Nash, the very person they were attempting to free. J. Edgar Hoover used this bold and violent raid as the basis for his push to strengthen the power of the FBI.

A mark on the wall at the entrance to Union Station was thought to have been made by a bullet fired during the Kansas City Massacre. Evidence has now disproved that theory.

There are markings on the front wall of Union Station where the massacre took place that for a long time people believed to be bullet holes from the shootout. After testing by law enforcement, it has been determined that the markings were not caused by bullets at all. However, the legend lives on, and a plaque stands next to the markings on the wall to commemorate the peace officers that gave their lives in the line of duty that day.

Frank Nash, criminal and escaped prisoner, was shot and killed just a few feet outside the Union Station by the very people who came to free him. Considering such a violent death at the hands of his own men, it would be no surprise if Frank Nash's spirit was unable to rest and indeed lingers on in a state of limbo, haunting Kansas City's Union Station.

"Ghosts only exist

for those who wish to see them."

—Holtei

33

The Elms Resort and Spa

Gamblers, coal workers, housekeepers, mobsters, and mothers.

What is the common thread among these characters? They are all spirits that have made their presence known at the famous Elms Resort and Spa in Excelsior Springs, Missouri.

Originally built in the 1880s, the Elms has been rebuilt twice due to fires that burned the hotel to the ground each time. The structure standing today was opened to the public, with much fanfare, on September 7, 1912.

Since that time, the luxurious resort has seen a varied clientele. The Elms Resort claims that during Prohibition, Al Capone, "Pretty Boy" Floyd, and Bugsy Moran reportedly hosted illegal gambling and bathtub gin parties at the resort. It is said that police tried to raid the Elms during Prohibition on several occasions, but the raids were unsuccessful because the suspects were warned ahead of time.

Questionable, underground activities seemed to be quite prevalent during those times. One of the spirits hanging around the Elms is supposedly a gambler involved in illegal activities. It is said he met an untimely death during the speakeasy days of Prohibition and now haunts the lap pool area in the basement where he lost his life. There are also reports of mysterious phone calls to the front desk. It seems the calls originate from within the hotel in rooms that are empty!

In 1948, the hotel hosted Harry S. Truman the night of the presidential election. He and key members from his campaign party awaited the results from the election that most historians claim was the biggest upset in American history. He stayed in what is now room 300. The following morning, he traveled to his election headquarters in Kansas

The Elms Resort and Spa, in Excelsior Springs, is reportedly haunted by several resident spirits.

City to accept his victory and returned to the Elms that night amid a media frenzy. Although no one claims to have seen President Truman's ghost at the resort, his impression lives on in the Truman Suite.

One not-so-famous guest has been seen as an apparition in the basement. The spirit of a woman has been known to throw things and pull hair. Her story, however, is not known. Some people say she died searching for her missing child during one of the early fires at the site of the hotel and continues her search even in the afterlife.

Another fire-related legend is that of two coal shovelers who were killed in the basement where they were working when the hotel caught fire during a Halloween masquerade ball in 1910. Legend says that if you hear the clanging of pipes around 1:30 AM, the time of the fire, it just might be one of those past workers.

No fatalities were officially reported from either fire at the Elms Resort, so the true stories remain a mystery. There is still no explanation for the strange experiences that are attributed to these spirits.

The final ghost is that of a housekeeper from another era. This maid's apparition has been seen on the 3rd floor and appears to be wearing an old-fashioned uniform from around the 1920s time period.

Over the years, the Elms Resort and Spa has had a wide array of visitors from all walks of life. It is no wonder, with such a rich and storied past, that the grand hotel would have visitors from other dimensions as well.

Back view of the stately hotel.

A hauntingly beautiful view of the grounds around the Elms Resort.

34

Hall of Waters

The Hall of Waters was at one time the world's largest mineral bar, offering a variety of soda, iron, manganese, and calcium waters.

If everyone has gone home for the night, why are lights flashing through the halls?

If the swimming pool on the ground floor is closed, why are splashing noises coming from there?

Built in 1935 as a health destination, the Hall of Waters now houses government offices as well as a museum.

These are questions many people ask about the strange happenings at the Hall of Waters in Excelsior Springs, Missouri (about 40 miles northeast of Kansas City). But no one quite knows the answer.

The Hall of Waters was built in 1935 when ten mineral springs were tapped to create a resort. The structure hosted the world's longest mineral water bar and health spa. Besides the bar, there was also a 30' x 75' swimming pool, a women's bath department, a sunroom, a covered porch, and a grand foyer. Next to the pool was a hydrotherapy section devoted to researching ways to use water in the treatment of various chronic illnesses.

The cost for the building, totaling more than 1 million dollars, was funded through President Roosevelt's Works Progress Administration (WPA) project # 5252.

Deep into the Great Depression of the 1930s, President Roosevelt and Congress created an initiative called the WPA. (After 1939, WPA came to stand for Works Projects Administration.) The WPA was in integral part of the President's New Deal program and was created in an effort to assist the hundreds of thousands of out-of-work Americans.

Times were so tough that people were literally wandering the streets looking for work. This work program gave Americans something to feel proud of and provided a way to put a little money back into the economy. Some critics claimed that money and time were wasted because some of the projects were overly labor-intensive and inefficient. But the purpose was to get as many Americans working as quickly as possible and for that, the WPA served its purpose well.

As a result of the program, many public buildings, roads, parks and playgrounds were constructed and still stand today—especially in rural communities. In the area around Kansas City, the majority of labor-intensive work used indigenous rock and stone. One such job was building the Hall of Waters. Today, the building serves as City Hall for Excelsior Springs and is on the National Register of Historic Places.

Maybe it is the spirit of one of those struggling workers who flickers the lights in the Hall of Waters late at night, thinking their work is not quite finished. And what about the splashing noises in the ground level pool? Could it possibly be a health spa guest returning from the afterlife? It is hard to say for sure what causes the strange lights and sounds of the Hall of Waters, but it does not appear to be anyone living in this century.

Just down the road is Roosevelt School, also reported to be haunted. The stonework, similar to the Hall of Waters, was built through the WPA.

Unexplainable noises are heard and lights are seen at the Hall of Waters in Excelsior Springs.

35

The Pink Rosebud Bed and Breakfast

It was early October in historic Plattsburg, Missouri. Red and orange leaves were scattered across the lawn, lying for a moment where the wind had blown them. The heat of the day was fading away as the cooler night air crept up the street over the old Victorian homes and restored Historical Museum next door.

Two couples sat relaxing on the stone porch of the Pink Rosebud Bed and Breakfast decompressing from a long day at the ballpark. They had come to watch the Kansas City Royals play the Minnesota Twins in the major league playoffs. Drinks in hand, the couples were winding down.

Inside the beautifully restored home, owner John Huffman and his wife busied themselves with putting their Bed and Breakfast to sleep for the night. Dessert had been served, and with their guests relaxing on the front porch, all was quiet and calm.

Suddenly, astonished shouts were heard out front! Worried that something was wrong, John hurried to see what had happened. As he reached the front door, he sensed Rosa float past him. "Oh, it's just Rosa coming in for the night and having a little fun with my guests," he thought, relieved. He ventured out to the porch to quiet his guests and hear what they thought of his resident spirit.

The Pink Rosebud Bed and Breakfast, in Plattsburg, Missouri, hosts a variety of spirits year-round.

The excited guests explained to John that as they sat on the wide overhung porch, the apparition of a woman suddenly appeared on the manicured lawn in front of them. But she did not look quite right. She floated just off of the ground and was dressed in clothes from another century. Her murky image glided directly toward the group, seeming to look through them. She breezed directly over their heads and in through the front door, then rose smoothly up the steps.

As the group walked inside, still talking excitedly, Mr. Huffman and his bewildered guests saw Rosa poised at the top of the staircase in front of them. She was looking back to survey the group with a glare as if they were the ones intruding into her domain, not the other way around.

This was not the first time Rosa had made her presence known in the quaint and beautifully restored 1878 stone home. A woman of color, she was nanny to the children of the Phillips family that had previously owned the home. It is thought the timeframe was in the 1920s and possibly into the 30s. As would be expected of someone in charge of energetic children who roamed everywhere, Rosa has been seen all over the grounds--in the yard and throughout the home at all times of day.

Rosa's presence can also be felt in other ways. Her rose-scented perfume, not the freshest (it actually smells quite bad), can be detected at the most unexpected times. John says that he has often entered a room where no one has been recently and can smell Rosa's namesake perfume permeating the space.

Rosa has also been known to decorate—or redecorate. John states that several times he has been setting the table, left to get something else, and found items rearranged on the table upon his return! He has not yet seen Rosa doing this. It actually could be one of the other two 'permanent' guests at the Bed and Breakfast—a young man and a grey cat, both long since deceased!

Rumor has it that a Mr. Morgan, accused of murder in the 1890s, is the ghostly young man seen occasionally at The Pink Rosebud B & B. He hung himself a week before his trial at another location, but the young man's body was laid out and the funeral was held for him at the house that is now The Pink Rosebud B & B. While this spirit would not be considered malicious, his actions can be a little more invasive and alarming to those not used to this behavior.

Mr. Morgan is seen most often in the three rooms upstairs. Guests of the B & B have reported being awakened with an eerie feeling of being watched. Upon opening their eyes, they see a form of a young man standing over their bed. Beds have also been shaken, doors opened and closed, televisions turned on and off, and television channels changed. These events, at the very least, result in quite interesting conversations around the breakfast table the next morning!

The final haunting resident of the Pink Rosebud is a large grey cat. This ghost usually affects the living family cats in residence. At times these felines get quite upset about something in the room no one else can see. They hiss and arch their backs to show their displeasure at the intrusion. When the Huffmans or guests investigate, they often spy a grey tail trailing around a corner out of the room. As soon as the ghost is gone, the family cats relax again. No one is sure whom the cat originally belonged to, but the Huffmans think of it as theirs now. This grey feline ghost is most often seen in the dining room and kitchen. It seems even spirit cats like hanging around the food!

The beautifully restored 1878 Pink Rosebud Bed and Breakfast has stories to tell.

So how do the Huffmans deal with living among the non-living? Actually, they have found a way to live together in harmony. If the inn is particularly busy, and the ghosts are up to their tricks and getting in the way, the Huffmans just state firmly "Go away, we're too busy right now!" And the spirits seem to obey!

The Pink Rosebud Bed and Breakfast is located at 500 S. Birch Ave in Plattsburg, Missouri, 30 miles north of Kansas City. www. pinkrosebudbnb.com

36

Plattsburg Historical Museum

Plattsburg, Missouri, located north of Kansas City and close to Smithville Lake, is a county-seat town. It has an old-world charm enhanced by the beautifully restored Victorian homes situated along tree-lined streets, especially along Clay Avenue. Founded in 1833, 2008 marked the town's 175th anniversary.

The Riley-Carmack House and Museum, located next to the Pink Rosebud B & B, contains the Plattsburg Historical Museum. The building was built in 1888 and recently restored by the Historical Society. The museum is rumored to contain more than the wonderful historical items from the area's past, however: a ghost!

It is thought that the matriarchal ghost of the last family to own the home, Lady Carmack, remains within its walls. The spirit of Lady Carmack has been known to rattle around the museum at odd times of day and night, causing unexplained noises and rustling sounds that surprise Historical Society volunteers and visitors to the museum. Rarely seen, she is a friendly ghost who makes her presence known through a cold, eerie feeling a person gets when sharing space with a spirit.

The Riley-Carmack House and Museum may have more than historical items on display.

Graceful Victorian homes can be seen throughout historic Plattsburg, Missouri.

Chances are good that more ghost stories are waiting to be heard about some of the old homes in Plattsburg.

Plattsburg is a wonderful town filled with people dedicated to preserving its glorious past. If traveling through, be sure to head up and down a few of the tree-lined streets to spy some awesome old homes. It's a good bet that several of them have their own ghost stories to tell as well.

37

The Haunted Noland Family

Do spirits choose when and where they haunt? Can they transfer from one channel of communication to another—say from haunting a car to a house? The members of the Noland family, who live south of Kansas City, believe that they can.

In 2004, Mr. and Mrs. Noland bought a beat-up Ford Escort for their son, Brian. The car looked like it could fall apart any day, and Brian was glad every time it started. Almost immediately after receiving his gift, Brian began noticing strange things. While driving, Brian would feel a pressure on the back of his driver's seat. It felt exactly like someone was sitting close behind him with their knees pressed firmly into the seat. It was not a constant pressure either; it would vary in intensity and location on the seat as though the unseen passenger was adjusting to get more comfortable.

This occurrence was disturbing because it happened when Brian was alone in his car. There was no reasonable explanation that he could come up with. After a few weeks, Brian noticed that a strange gelatinous substance would appear on the back seat and the ceiling of the car. He would clean it off, but the gel would reappear the next day. It did not have a smell and did not appear to be anything gruesome like blood—but combined with the pressure against the back of the driver's seat, Brian

was a little unsettled. He was convinced that he had acquired
a ghost along with his new car.

The rest of the Noland family was hesitant to believe there
was anything out of the ordinary happening; Brian could be
a bit eccentric at times. He actually seemed excited about his
new friend (as they began to call the spirit) and encouraged it
to show itself. Then one day, the strange occurrences in his car
stopped abruptly. Brian was both relieved and disappointed—he
kind of liked the idea of a haunted car!

The Noland family assumed the Escort spirit, if there ever
was one, had left and that was that. They soon found out,
however, that they were only partially correct. It seemed that
the spirit had indeed decided to abandon the traveler's life
and no longer haunted Brian's car. But they were shocked to
discover that it chose to settle down in a nice home instead.
The Noland home!

This realization came first to the family's grandmother,
Nana. Nana was an unyielding 86-year-old Italian woman. Her
relatives joked that Nana had lived on a hot dog and coffee
diet for the last twelve years. They could all safely say that
she was not a big believer in the supernatural--but that would
soon change.

One evening, Nana finished her nightly activity of sewing
throw blankets (in between short naps in her rocking chair) and
decided it was time for bed. She climbed into bed and was soon
sound asleep. Several hours into the night, Nana was roused
from slumber by the feel of tapping on her leg, just above her
ankle. She initially assumed it was her daughter and looked
towards the foot of the bed preparing to ask sharply "What do
you want?" As the elderly woman's eyes focused, however, she
realized it was not her daughter, but a very tall woman Nana
had never seen before. The specter had long black hair which
fell wildly past her shoulders and was dressed in a flowing white
dress. Her face was indiscernible--just a pale blur covered by
jet black hair.

Nana, slightly panicked, rolled over and curled up. She
pulled the blankets up to her chin and hoped fervently that she
had been dreaming. Fortunately, she drifted back to sleep and
was not bothered again for the remainder of the night. The next
morning at the breakfast table, her family's alarmed reaction
mirrored her own sense of uneasiness about her encounter the
previous evening. Could the black-haired spirit have sought

out the one person in the house most adamant about the non-existence of ghosts? What did she want, and why would she wake Nana only to allow her to go back to sleep? The other members of the family (except Brian, of course) all hoped they would not be next on the ghost's nightly visitation schedule. But they did not get their wish because a few weeks later the spirit visited another occupant of the Noland family home.

Brian's girlfriend Eddie was in bed sound asleep with one leg stretched out of the covers. Her foot was hanging slightly off the bed, and she felt a gentle brushing across the bottom of it, along her arch. It was a very light tickling sensation and was not quite enough to completely awaken her. It did, however, spark her awareness of the sounds around her. As she felt the next "tickle," she heard a woman giggling. Eddie fought the urge to pull her leg in under the covers because at first, she thought it was a family member playing a prank. She knew that if they succeeded in spooking her she would never hear the end of it! Everyone was a little edgy after all the supernatural occurrences, and she would not put it past someone to try to scare her good-naturedly. But then her sleepy brain registered something alarming. There were no other family members in the house except Brian, and he was sound asleep right next to her! Immediately, she tucked her foot in and under the covers. What a strange and eerie experience to hear a ghost giggling as it tickled her foot in the middle of the night!

One night, Lance, a friend of the family, stayed the night on the couch. As he lie sleeping facing the back of the sofa, he felt firm pressure on his exposed side. He woke up and turned to see who was trying to wake him, but no one was there. As he tried to go back to sleep, he heard a ghostly whisper call out "Lance" several times. Lance whipped his head around trying to find the source of the voice, but could find no one in the vicinity.

These were not the only ways that the Noland family ghost made herself known. She also liked to cause what the family called the 'mystery thump.' On a fairly regular basis, for no apparent reason, they would hear a very loud clunk. The bizarre aspect to this 'thump' was that no one could ever pin down the origin of the sound. One time, Scott, Brian's brother, was in his room downstairs with his fiancée when they heard the noise. They were sure the sound had come from upstairs, but when they went to investigate, they saw Mr. and Mrs. Noland looking down at them. Scott's parents were sure the thump came from downstairs! Each time it happened, all parties would leave their respective rooms to investigate and ensure everyone was ok. It was a comical sight with Scott looking up the stairs, his parents looking down the stairs, and everyone wondering about the source of the sound.

One evening, the Nolands were visiting and talking about their ghost. Even with the mounting evidence of ghostly activities other family members had experienced, Scott still had his doubts about whether it was really a spirit behind it all. He joked that he did not believe in such things and teased Brian about his staunch support of the haunted house theory. Brian retorted that everyone should be careful because 'his' ghost did not like anyone picking on him. Scott self-confidently replied "So what, I'm not afraid of her. Bring it on!" What could happen, right?

That very same night Scott went downstairs to bed, the family ghost the farthest thing from his mind. Around 3:00 a.m. (he looked at the clock later), Scott was abruptly awakened with a pinch on his backside! Believing it was his fiancée being funny, he sat up and looked in her direction. But she was facing the other way, sound asleep, and the bed had not moved. She could not have been the culprit. As he sat there in bed wondering what had just happened, Scott got the overwhelming feeling that there was someone in the room behind him at the head of his bed. His skin crawled because it felt as if he were being watched. He debated for several moments whether to even turn around. Finally, he turned to look. Nothing but darkness greeted his tired eyes. More awake and alert now, Scott decided to check his door, thinking it was possible his brother was pulling a prank. However, his door was still shut and locked. At that precise moment, Scott became a firm believer in the existence of the Noland family ghost.

The Nolands experienced no further activity from the dark-haired poltergeist for another two months. Mr. Noland was up in his room working a crossword puzzle when he heard "I'm back." Assuming it was his wife, Pat, he nodded his head and finished the crossword. About ten minutes later he went looking for Pat, but could not find her anywhere. He ventured into Nana's room and asked her if she knew where Pat was because he heard her say she was back. Nana replied that Pat was not in the house and would not be back for a while. The only explanation the family could come up with was that their ghost had returned after taking a vacation of sorts.

The last time the Noland family heard from their ghost was on Christmas that year. The house was packed with family and friends, and everyone was having a good time. A large group was in the dining area adjacent to the kitchen, and others were downstairs in the family room and in the poolroom. As the group in the dining area was talking, a large bowl resting on a ledge above the cabinets suddenly flew from its perch and fell to the floor with a bang and clatter. Everyone stopped talking and looked at one another. How had that happened? That bowl had been there for years, and nothing had fallen from that ledge since the house was built. The bowl had been sitting on the cabinets that hung over the refrigerator, but on its way down, it strangely didn't bounce on anything. It actually landed about three feet away from the refrigerator. It seemed as if the bowl had been thrown from the ledge.

The last person to go into the kitchen that night was a cousin, Kim. She and a friend had been discussing the Noland family ghost, and Kim had said sharply that if the ghost was there, she should leave the house. Kim walked out of the kitchen and mere moments later the bowl flew off the cabinets. Seemingly, the angry ghost took Kim's advice, and the Noland family never heard from their specter again.

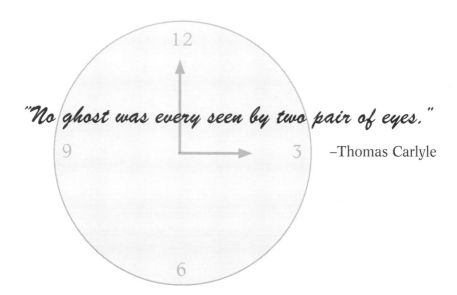

"No ghost was every seen by two pair of eyes."

–Thomas Carlyle

38

Longview Farm

World-renowned equestrian, animal lover, lumber heiress, and philanthropist: Loula Long Combs, lived all these roles at the beautiful Longview Mansion and Farm near Lee's Summit, Missouri. Could she also be called a ghostly specter? Many people believe that she, Queen of the American Royal, still lingers about the estate.

Sue, a student at nearby Longview Community College, was walking from campus to her car in the parking lot. She had stayed late to finish a project for the night class she was taking and only a few other cars were sprinkled around the lot. As she approached her trusty Grand Am, Sue heard a muffled sound—a sort of drumming. Her heart beat rapidly and she positioned her keys in her hand to defend herself. Looking around the well-lit lot, however, Sue saw no one near her. She peaked under her car and peered in the windows to make sure no one was waiting to attack. Everything looked ok, and so shaking her head, she got into her car and pulled out of the lot.

Turning toward home, Sue maneuvered her car in the direction of Longview Farm. It was a warm summer night, and her car had no air conditioning. With the windows all down, Sue heard the loud chorus of the June bugs and then that drumming sound again. But this time, it was not as muffled. It sounded more like horse's hooves galloping on hard-packed earth. Not really a "clomp, clomp," but more of a "thud, thud," as the hooves hit dirt. Thinking it strange and a little unsafe that someone would go galloping along the road at night, Sue slowed down and pulled over to the side. Strangely, the sound did not grow louder or dissipate. It remained constant as it hung in the air for a few more moments and then was gone in a snap. Sue waited a while longer in the warm night. The sound of the June bugs again held sole possession of the night breeze, but neither horse nor rider ever journeyed past her.

In addition to hearing phantom pounding hooves, others in the area of Longview Farm (such as students at the college and visitors to Longview Lake) have reported seeing the filmy vision of a woman dressed in period clothing sitting atop a magnificent horse. Once spotted, these apparitions seem to gently fade away as if on a breeze.

Born in 1881, Loula Long Combs loved horses at an early age. Luckily, her father's successful lumber business provided the means to support her expensive equine interests. Noted for her hard work and self-discipline, Loula soon became a noted sportswoman and participated in events well into her old age. Indeed, she was the only woman to be inducted by the horse-show world into the Madison Square Garden Hall of Fame. In addition to her horses, Loula loved all animals, and it is said she took in any stray dog that appeared on her land. Loula also continued the philanthropy for which her father was so well known. In 1964, Loula and her older sister Sally America Long Ellis donated 147 acres of Longview Farm for the creation of Longview Community College.

Built between 1913 and 1914 by lumber baron Robert A. Long, Longview Farm encompassed more than 1700 acres and 40 buildings. It sported a half-mile racetrack with grandstand and clubhouse as well. Whitewashed post and fencing encircled the entire country estate. Mr. Long also built a 50-room mansion on the grounds, and when Loula married Robert Pryer Combs on July 30, 1917, the couple soon took up residence in it. It was there they stayed for the remainder of their lives. Loula died in 1971, but it is speculated that her spirit remains on the estate.

In 1987, Longview Mansion was chosen as the Symphony Designers Showhouse. During that time, it was reported that every morning Loula's bed had to be remade. Was this strange occurrence due to a ghostly presence or a staff member's prank? The answer to that question still remains a mystery.

Longview Farm operated as a working horse and stock farm. The estate was well known for its pure bred Jersey dairy cattle and prize-winning greenhouse. And of course, the farm provided Loula with more than enough room to breed, train and show her horses. In fact, her most beloved mount, Revelation, was buried in front of the Longview Show Horse Arena. Perhaps Revelation is the mysterious steed that has been both seen and heard on quiet evenings, deep into the night around the Farm.

39

A Whistling Stranger

Emporia, Kansas, just south of Kansas City, has an apartment complex that was once an old hospital. The areas that made up the working hospital were all converted into living spaces. For example, the hospital's basement morgue is now a storage area. The chapel was converted into a unique apartment where the living room boasts *true* cathedral ceilings that continue into the kitchen and a raised area directly opposite the front door was once the altar. The chapel's confessional was turned into a bathroom. The stained glass windows were removed from the 'chapel apartment' and placed on display in the entryway to the four-story Hillcrest building.

This apartment complex became home for two college roommates. Off and on throughout Kim and Meredith's stay in the building, they experienced many odd occurrences. As a rule, they attributed the flickering lights, eerie creaks, and strange sounds to an old building and its faulty wiring. Looking at it in this way was the best way to keep their sanity. Their only other option was to admit that the building was haunted! On one occasion, however, the events that transpired were just too strange to explain away with flimsy excuses.

Meredith was in the apartment alone one night while Kim was visiting her family for the weekend. Meredith was in the living room watching television when she heard whistling coming from inside Kim's room. It was not a monotone whistle like you would hear from electronic equipment; it was a human whistling sound. The whistler was attempting a tune, although Meredith could not identify it. It sounded as though someone was lying on Kim's bed whistling—just patiently waiting for her to return.

Meredith had not left the apartment all night, so she assured herself that there was no way anyone could have entered without her knowledge. "Or was there?" she thought. Tentatively, Meredith stepped toward the room and knocked. There was no answer, but the whistling stopped, so she peeked inside. The room was empty.

Completely horrified, Meredith quickly left the apartment to gain composure. She could only hope the spirit would be gone by the time she returned. The next afternoon, Kim returned from her family visit to find her friend completely on edge. As soon as Kim entered the apartment, Meredith insisted she go into her room and check the messages on her answering machine. She needed to find out who or what had left such a creepy message—a message filled with a tuneless, but eerie whistle!

Kim saw that her friend was totally spooked and felt goose bumps appear on her arms. Entering her room, she pushed the blinking message indicator light on her answering machine. What had happened to spook her friend so thoroughly? Kim mentally shook off the unnerving feelings and pushed the button to retrieve the message.

The familiar sound of a friend's voice came from the machine. "Sorry I missed you. Give me a call when you get this." The answering machine beeped and then sat silently. There was no eerie whistling message.

Kim glanced at Meredith and the expression on her friend's face really alarmed her. What exactly had happened last night? As Meredith explained to Kim what she had experienced, she stated that the only way she had made it through the night was by convincing herself that the sound was just an answering machine message--not a voice from beyond the grave. If it had not been a person in the apartment that night, then what exactly made the whistling noise? The only plausible answer Meredith had come up with was that someone had called (even though she had not heard the phone ring) and left a message. But that theory didn't seem to have merit.

Had it been a failed attempt at humor from a playful friend? A joke that just did not get recorded on the answering machine? Or did the hauntingly eerie sounds emanate from a more disturbing source?

Kim and Meredith believe it may have been the spirit of a long-since-departed individual from the hospital, a patient who may have stayed in the room that now held Kim's possessions. Perhaps it was someone who had given his last confession in what is now the bathroom just down the hall!

40

Christian Church Hospital

In the dead of night several years ago, a police officer and his partner were called to an old abandoned building at 27th and West Paseo in Kansas City, Missouri. Teenagers with flashlights were walking around the unsafe structure past midnight, and the policemen asked them to leave. That summer, there had been an unusually high number of groups wandering about the place after dark. To understand the reason for so many nocturnal visitors, the officers asked some of the teens what they were doing at the building. The teens told them there was an urban legend about the place. The vacant building had once been a smallpox hospital (*my research could not confirm this*), and the souls of patients who had died in the place were everywhere. If the place was haunted, then they wanted to find some ghosts!

Their story intrigued one officer, Rich, and he decided to do a little ghost hunting himself. After gaining permission to take a look around, Rich and some friends went into the building around midnight a few nights later. Upon entering, the group could feel a presence in the vacant building. Rich was used to 'things that go bump in the night' and was not easily rattled. But there was something about the place, something not quite right. It had raised the hairs on the back of his neck and enveloped him in a particularly eerie sensation.

As he entered the gutted fifth floor, he noted that the windows were all broken or missing; it seemed as though they had been blown out by strong winds, yet he felt confined in the empty space. It seemed that many people were pressed together with him, but only his small group of friends were present.

Ghost stories about the Christian Church Hospital have been floating around for years, scaring youths throughout the city.

They knew the basement was where the morgue had been, and the group contemplated searching there, but no one that night was interested in going to the basement to see ghosts. They called it a night and left.

A few weeks later, the group returned with a digital camera at the request of Rich's wife, Melissa. On that second excursion, the officer took several photographs in and around the abandoned hospital and captured what appeared to be little circles of light in several of them. Not every picture had the orbs, even when they were taken in the same area, so they could not have been from a lightbulb or flash. Those involved feel certain that Rich captured ghost lights on film that night. Could the orbs be the spirits of long ago patients who never left the hospital?

Built between 1914 and 1916, the seven-story structure was founded by the Disciples of Christ as a private hospital for veterans and the poor. It served in this humble capacity for years, helping many in need. The Christian Church Hospital closed in 1926 and was then sold to the federal government. It was used for a short time by the Veteran's Administration.

In 1935, Dr. George W. Robinson, Sr. purchased the building and renamed it the Robinson Neurological Hospital. It was here that work was done in the area of addiction and mental disease. Bizarre rumors have claimed that some of the methods used for treating mental illness involved the use of chains, cages, wet sheets, beatings and the ice pick method of frontal lobotomies. These statements have not been substantiated by any of my research, but they definitely add to the creepiness of the place!

The hospital closed in the mid-1970s and sat abandoned for many years. Just recently renovated and redeveloped, the Christian Church Hospital is now known as the Residences of West Paseo. It houses 46 affordable senior living apartments and received a 2007 Preservation Award from the Historic Kansas City Foundation for its dedication to preserving the city's historic architecture and cultural landscapes.

Through its years of vacancy, the old hospital has been the topic of many ghostly tales. Figures and murky visions have been seen through the windows on several of the floors on dark spooky nights. It is said that hundreds of orbs surround the building and can be easily captured on camera at night. Could these images be the spirits of poor souls treated at the hospital and whose bodies have long since departed from this world?

41

The Flower

Many people have experiences that defy conventional wisdom: a rush of emotion, the feeling that someone is present in an empty room, objects moving without explanation. These experiences are sometimes centered around specific locations, such as a family home. This is the case for the Metrokotsas family at their home south of Kansas City. They built the house and it has remained in their possession for thirty years. It is a comfortable place where friends and family (both living and deceased) feel free to come and go as they please. The next two stories are theirs.

Kim entered her room and immediately noticed something was out of place. A single dried carnation was lying in the middle of floor—far away from where it was when she had left earlier that day.

"Ok, who's messing with my stuff?" was the teenager's first thought.

Kim bent down and retrieved the flower from its resting spot on the carpet. Strangely, the dried petals were all intact--which seemed impossible considering the flower had just that morning been woven tightly into the big wicker chair in the corner of her room. There was no way a person could pull it out without crumbling the petals or at least causing several of them to fall off. But nothing else was around the flower on the floor to indicate a mess had been created and then cleared away.

Kim's skin crawled as she looked around her room. Nothing else was out of place. Just the empty spot on her wicker chair where that carnation used to reside. How had the flower gotten five feet away into the middle of the room? It could not have just fallen on its own because it was too far away and had been woven into the wicker. Shaking off the eerie feelings creeping up on her, Kim bounded down the stairs to ask her family if anyone had been in her room that afternoon. It had to be one of her siblings messing around!

At her questioning, everyone denied even entering her room, much less doing anything with the flower. A pest control company had been in the house that day, but everyone seriously doubted one of the workers would move any such object.

Kim's mother could tell her daughter was bothered by the incident, so she asked why. "It's just weird," Kim said. "It was the flower from Grandpa's grave." Kim had almost a dozen dried roses woven through the chair from various occasions, but only one carnation...and it held great significance for her.

Her mom's face paled as she shook her head in disbelief. "Kim! Today is the anniversary of your grandfather's death," she exclaimed. They were talking about Kim's maternal grandfather, so her mother was especially affected by this possible message from the spiritual world. Mother and daughter looked at one another and silently agreed that something out of the ordinary was going on—something otherworldly.

Throughout his life, Kim's grandpa had been a quiet, stoic man. He loved and cared for his family, but he was not the type to get sentimental or show much emotion. While Kim had loved him tons, she was never sure exactly how close they were. Could the flower have been a sign that Grandpa appreciated the assistance everyone was giving his beloved wife, Nana? Was he, in his own quiet way, trying to encourage them to continue?

Even though the incident was unsettling, it left Kim with a good feeling inside. She believed it was a caring message sent from a loved patriarch watching over his family.

42

The Picture

At an impromptu family gathering one evening a few years later, something momentous happened that none of those involved will soon forget.

Kim Metrokotsas, her two sisters, and their mother were gathered around the kitchen table reminiscing about their grandmother who had passed on some years earlier. They were sorting through a box of their matriarch's old trinkets one by one. Many of Nana's possessions had interesting stories attached, and the women were having a good time retelling them.

Many objects were silly knickknacks collected by their eccentric Nana throughout her life. For example, they discovered a small metal camel charm, and if there was any sentimental value to it, none of the girls knew what it could have been. They laughed hysterically at some of the odd-ball items in the collection. Suddenly, through the laughter, they all heard a crash in the other room.

Since no one else was home and it did not sound like a door closing, the laughter ceased immediately. The girls' mom told them to stay put as she headed into the other room to investigate. When they heard laughing from the other room, they ran in to join their giggling mother. On the floor below a shelf was a picture that had obviously toppled off and was the cause of the noise they had heard. As their mom picked it up and turned it over, the girls understood why she found this humorous instead of being concerned that a picture had flown off the shelf. It was a picture of Nana.

There was no logical explanation for the incident. The cabinet could not have been bumped by anything (no cats, dogs, or persons were in the room), and no other photo frames on the shelf had been disturbed. Was this a mystical communication from a cherished ancestor or simply an eerie mishap?

The girls have no doubt that their experience was a brush with their grandmother's ghost. They still believe to this day that the spirit of their beloved Nana was reaching out to them. Either she wanted to be included in the fun and happiness of the moment, or she was irritated that they were poking fun of her collectibles! Nevertheless, with all the history and memories within the Metrokotsas home, it is likely this will not be the last time the location is used for beyond-the-grave contact.

"Behind every man now alive stands thirty ghosts, for that is the ratio by which the dead outnumber the living."

—Arthur C. Clarke

43

Aliens in the Prairie

Aunt Beulah never told a lie in her entire life. That is why, after more than a decade of silence, no one doubted her story when she finally shared it.

It was summer in the country. Far enough away from Kansas City that the only lights that could be seen were those coming from the lightning bugs around their farm. Aunt Beulah and Uncle Robin were relaxing on their porch swing when they saw an airplane flying above them. Strangely, it appeared to be flying *toward* them, rather than over them!

Alarmed, they stood up and walked out into the yard to get a better view. They also hoped to have more room to maneuver away if necessary. The craft was long, like a cigar, and about the size of a school bus. They noticed little windows along the side like it was a passenger plane of some sort. But it did not look like or act like any sort of airplane that they knew of.

The spaceship (that's really the only explanation they could come up with) approached them slowly and hovered just above their heads. It appeared to be looking them over. Then, as if deciding these two little humans standing alone out in the country were no threat to them, the ship took off and was gone in a split second.

It took Aunt Beulah many years to ever share her story. Back in the 1940s, the tale would probably not have been well-received. Although cautious about whom she told, Aunt Beulah did not hesitate to stay true to the story and defend her impressions of that night.

Nowadays, there are many reports of cigar-shaped spaceship sightings. Traditionally, the standard depiction of UFOs was a saucer-shaped object. What could the flying object have been? Did this couple see visitors from outer-space that night on their lawn? We may never know.

44

The King's Ghost

Rich King's ancestors built a home in the northeast part of Kansas City over one hundred years ago. The home has stayed in the family all of this time, and Rich visited it often growing up. It has been the location of many supernatural occurrences.

As children visiting their grandparents, Rich and his brother would often be relegated to the upstairs bedroom for sleeping. The nighttime activities of ghostly occupants of the house were so numerous that the children started to ignore them after a while. Rich became so accustomed to the supernatural incidents that sometimes, if he was really tired, he would just lie in bed and pretend to be asleep. "I'm sleeping, I'm sleeping," became a sort of mantra.

One particularly shocking incident stands out above all the rest for Rich. He was about 10 years old and playing upstairs in a room that he did not go into very often. It was a catch-all type room with a lot of sewing materials, knick knacks, and other items that were hard to store. Rich was messing around with a stapler that he had discovered when he accidentally stapled his hand. He hollered in pain and fright when he saw the staple sticking out of his hand. Blood was oozing from the puncture. Cradling his hand in front of him, Rich ran down the stairs as fast as he could go. Family members met him at the bottom to see what was wrong, but when Rich uncovered his hand for them to examine, the staple was no longer stuck in his hand and there was no blood anywhere!

Most families would be a little freaked out when a young boy explained that a very painful injury just mysteriously disappeared, but not Rich's family. They just shook their heads and thought—"it's this house."

The sound of unaccounted-for footsteps was often heard by the King family at various times of the day throughout the house. One night, Rich heard footsteps coming up the stairs toward the room where he was trying to sleep. Tired of all the noises, he went to investigate and found no one on the stairs or anywhere near them. The sound stopped as he peered down the stairway.

Rich's cousin was also a magnet for the ghostly activity. It seemed to Rich that things happened to her more often than anyone else in the family. When she was staying in the house, her bed would shake, and doors would shut of their own volition.

At other times, family members experienced doors closing without the assistance of human hands. The family would also hear strange noises such as creaks, groans, and moans that could not be reasonably explained away. Indeed, the only reasonable explanation was that their house was haunted.

45

The Stranger

If you read a lot of ghost stories (or just this book), you will discover that not just places are haunted. Many times, individuals experience brushes with supernatural forces in a variety of ways. Rich King is one of those people, and following is one of his encounters with a ghostly specter as a young adult.

Rich was coming up the stairs from the basement of his mother's house to the main floor. As he completed his climb and turned to enter the family room, he glanced to his right out the front door window. There he spied a man in the driveway. He wore a brown flannel shirt and was standing next to Rich's car. The man's hands were on his hips, and he was sort of leaning to one side as if he was patiently waiting for someone to notice him.

"That is strange," Rich thought as he stepped back to look again. But this time when he looked, there was no one there. The apparition of the man whom Rich had seen standing by his car was no longer in sight.

As Rich thought more about what he had seen, he felt certain that the spirit of his grandfather, who had passed away the year before, had visited him that day. The specter, although filmy, looked like his grandfather and was of a similar height and build. He even wore a flannel shirt just like his grandfather had always worn.

Even though there was no specific reason for his grandfather's spirit to appear that day (it was not a significant day, and no one was in trouble—that sort of thing), Rich felt good to know that the connection to his family was still strong even after death. Theories abound as to why this happens, but generally, experts believe that some individuals are more open to seeing the world from an unfamiliar and sometimes spooky perspective.

46

Everlasting Love

Across the globe, people believe that a person's spirit is separated from their body at some point after death. I believe that most souls move along to a better place—another dimension you might say. However, it is the ones that seem to linger, often known as ghosts, spirits, specters, and apparitions that are most intriguing.

Why do souls linger or return to haunt the living? Theories abound, but the common thought is that there is a strong emotional link from a spirit to this world. Sometimes it is a violent or tragic death. Sometimes it is an unfinished task. And sometimes, it is love. Like my mother before me, I teach my children that love is forever, and that death cannot contain it. As such, I would like to share the following story about everlasting love.

A young couple, Beth and Tom, were ecstatic to discover that they would soon be expecting a little baby. But on the heels of that happy news came tragedy. Tom was diagnosed with terminal brain cancer. A few short days after holding his newborn son in his arms, he passed away.

Eventually, Beth remarried and found contentment with a good man. Together, Beth and Steve were raising a happy, healthy, and slightly rambunctious little boy.

One day, the little four-year-old boy was misbehaving, and Beth sent him to his room. As mothers do, she told him to lie on his bed and think about what he had done wrong. After a few minutes, Beth went into the youngster's room and asked him if he had thought about his actions.

The boy said, "Oh yes, Daddy came and sat on the bed with me. He told me that I should mind my mommy, and I should mind Daddy Steve because he loves me too."

Beth was astounded! It took a few minutes to find her voice, but she finally asked if he had talked to his daddy before. "Yes," replied her son, "he has come to talk with me a couple of other times. He usually tells me to mind you, and he always says how much he loves me."

"The distance that the dead have gone

Does not at first appear—

Their coming back seems possible

For many an ardent year."

—Emily Dickinson

Cemeteries

T he following poem has been seen on many gravestones around the world. The original author is unknown.

> "Come blooming youths, as you pass by,
> And on these lines, do cast an eye.
> As you are now, so once was I;
> As I am now, so must you be;
> Prepare for death and follow me."

An un-credited source wrote a humorous follow-up:

> "To follow you
> I am not content,
> How do I know
> Which way you went?"

Why do cemeteries seem to be haunted? Some people believe cemeteries are portals to other worlds beyond our familiar one. And we happen to spy so many spirits and ghostly figures because they are passing back and forth from our world to theirs through unseen gates within the burial ground.

It is sort of a numbers game, and it makes sense that there would be more ghosts seen at a cemetery than at any other type location. With such a high number of souls passing through, it would be surprising if a cemetery was not haunted!

What happens to our spirits after we die? Generally, stories surrounding death make us uneasy, even frightened. It is not surprising—the reality and often gruesome details that accompany cemetery stories can be pretty disturbing. Do you know what physically happens to our bodies in the ground after we are buried? Yuck! I believe that most of our fears, however, are based on the fact that no one knows for sure what happens to the essence of 'us.' It is the ultimate question. Some people believe that you die and that is that. Nothing mysterious happens. Others believe that our spirits go somewhere—heaven, hell, or somewhere in between. That 'somewhere in between' is when the conversation usually gets interesting!

Throughout history, people have often attached superstitions to the places where they bury their dead. Ancient Egyptians built whole pyramids simply to house their deceased. Through the ages, necessity, location, and priorities of the time all determined what societies did with those who passed on. Today, the most common options are to either bury loved ones in a cemetery where their resting place will be perpetually cared for or to cremate the body and then scatter or store the ashes in a purposeful or meaningful way.

There are all kinds of cemeteries: public and private, rural and urban. Cemeteries all exist to serve pretty much the same purpose—bury the dead. They also have something else in common—giving most people the creeps. Ghost stories go with cemeteries like spiders and their webs. Where you find one, you'll usually find the other.

Here's a quick look at some of the more well-known boneyards in the Kansas City area. Check them out, and let me know what you find!

Cemetery behind William Jewell College

On the edge of the campus of William Jewell College in Liberty, Missouri, sits a small old cemetery. Housed within its borders are several graves of children taken from this world too early. One graduate from the college reported that as a student, she and her friends would pass by the site on their way home from classes. They often felt a peculiar presence there.

One evening they visited the cemetery at midnight during a full moon to see if the haunted rumors were true. As they approached the cemetery, they spied the object of their adventure: Standing guard over one plot was the statue of a child. The eyes of the stone child glowed blue in the moonlight and to the girls, seemed very much alive!

Franklin Cemetery

If there is a full moon out, you may be able to spot lights flickering at the Franklin Cemetery in Liberty, Missouri. These ghostly illuminations are said to move across the graveyard in a pattern of sorts and then disappear.

Independence Cemetery

An old cemetery in Independence is reported to be haunted by Frontier ghosts. Some people have witnessed spooky flashing lights at night when no one is there. It is located in a residential area and is pretty run-down. Supposedly, there are graves dating back to the days of wagon trains when Independence was a popular jumping off point on the Oregon Trail. Are there ghosts of courageous pioneers still hovering in the area, their lanterns flickering in the dark?

Elmwood Cemetery

At Elmwood Cemetery on Truman Road in Kansas City, people have reported seeing the apparitions of two girls dressed in white. On cloudy days and nights, the little ghost girls can be seen playing together as if unaware that they are no longer alive and are in the middle of a cemetery.

Hill Park

This old cemetery in Independence houses the remains of Frank James, brother of outlaw Jesse James. Frank's wife, Ann Ralston, is also buried here. It has been reported that a Confederate soldier, killed during the battle at Independence in 1861, was laid to rest here and his spirit remains nearby. His grave is marked with an old stone marker. Visitors have reported seeing a filmy, ghostlike apparition moving over the hill and out of sight. Many believe it to be the spirit of the Confederate soldier.

Forest Hill Cemetery

Forest Hill Cemetery, at 6901 Troost Ave in Kansas City, holds many famous Kansas City legends. Satchel Page and Buck O'Neil, both Negro and Major League Baseball players, can be found alongside several other ball players. Tom Pendergast, Kansas City's infamous political boss, was laid to rest here as well. Both Confederate and Union officers, ironically, have been laid out in the same final resting place. Several strange stories surround the Forest Hill Cemetery.

One tale maintains that just as the sun dips below the horizon, music can be heard coming from inside one of the mausoleums. Another story says that a group of men's voices can be heard laughing and talking (the words are unclear) at various times throughout the night.

Union Cemetery

More than 55,000 people have been buried in Union Cemetery, located just south of Crown Center in Kansas City, Missouri. Many stories abound about this huge resting place. One resident of Union Hill reported seeing the apparition of a man walking slowly along the headstones. The man's head was down and his clothes appeared very shabby and dirty. Just as the resident was about to ask the apparition if he needed any help, he faded

One of the largest, Union Cemetery is believed to be the most haunted in the Kansas City area.

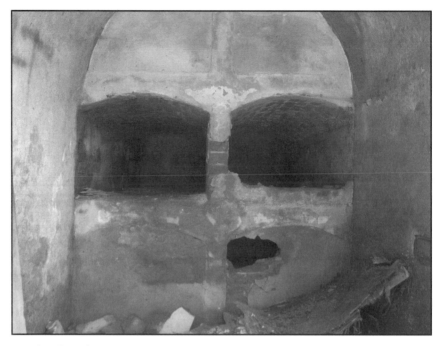

An abandoned crypt creates a spooky atmosphere in the Union Cemetery.

away into thin air. Many claims exist that there are cold spots all throughout the cemetery and that it is fairly easy to catch ghostly orbs with your digital camera.

"The fence around a cemetery is foolish,

for those inside can't get out

and those outside don't want to get in."

—Arthur Brisbane

Information for Ghost Hunters

The following information is provided by author and ghost investigator, Fiona Broome, from her book, Ghosts of Austin, Texas. *It is used here with permission. For more information, visit http:// hollowhill.com/.*

Guidelines for Ghost Hunters

1. **Use common sense.** If your "gut feeling" indicates that you're in danger, leave immediately. Ghost hunting shouldn't be dangerous, and it shouldn't be an endurance test, either.

2. **Never trespass.** If the site has "no trespassing" signs or looks as if it's closed, don't go in. Don't risk arrest.

3. **Take a friend with you when you go ghost hunting**. Never go to a quiet or deserted site alone, and never explore risky neighborhoods on your own.

4. **Dress for the setting.** Sturdy shoes are vital, especially if you're outdoors, or if you have to run to get away from a ghost.

5. Before visiting a location after dark, **see it in the daylight to check for hazards**, and things that might confuse you in lower light conditions.

6. **Never joke around cemeteries** or other haunted locations. That seems to offend the ghosts, and they can retaliate. Or, they may become obstinate and refuse to manifest.

7. Few ghosts appear as full figure apparitions. When they talk, it's often a garbled whisper. That's why we **record their "voices"** to study more carefully, later.

8. **Interact with the ghosts as if they're alive**. Be polite; they usually consider the location their personal property. Don't command them to manifest in a specific way. Unless they're ghosts of actors, they won't usually perform for anyone on cue.

9. **Ghosts don't follow you home**. If you're troubled by unwanted thoughts or feel uneasy after a ghost hunt, call a friend. Play your favorite music. Watch a funny TV show or movie. If dark or scary thoughts continue, consult your minister or spiritual advisor.

10. **Keep detailed notes** about your ghost hunts. Later, you'll find these notes very helpful, especially if you want to re-visit those haunted sites.

The following information is provided by author and ghost investigator, Fiona Broome and appears in her book, *Ghosts of Austin, Texas*.

For more information, visit http://hollowhill.com/.

Top Ten Places to Find Ghosts

No matter where you are, certain locations are usually haunted. These sites don't always have ghosts, but they're the best places to start when you're looking for unreported visitors from beyond the grave.

Theatres

Ghosts frequent places where people have performed on stage. These include movie theatres that were once performance halls.

There are three kinds of ghosts at these locations:

First, at least one actor who is still seen on or near the stage.

Second, a stagehand lingers backstage, usually around the lighting or the curtain controls.

Finally, someone appears towards the back of the hall, especially during rehearsals. He or she almost always smokes a cigarette that people can smell, or they'll see the smoke or the burning ember.

Battlegrounds

Almost every battleground has some residual energy from the violent and tragic deaths that occurred there. Some battlegrounds are actually haunted by the spirits of the men and women who died there, too. Between Texas' battles for independence, Indian attacks, and Civil War conflicts, you'll find many locations with ghost stories... and real ghosts.

Cemeteries

It's a cliché but a true one: Ghosts haunt cemeteries. Modern graves—burials that occurred less than fifty years ago—are rarely haunted for very long.

For the most powerful hauntings, look for graves that are at least a hundred years old. Only a few are haunted, but you'll find elevated EMF levels at many of graves, especially if they're unmarked.

Colleges

Almost every college or university reports at least one ghost. Most also report poltergeist phenomena. The performing arts center is often the most haunted location on campus. In Austin, the University of Texas campus is probably the most haunted college.

Summer Camps

Most camps—especially Scout camps—have a ghost or two. Usually, these are benevolent ghosts of former camp counselors or the camp manager. An aroma of perfume or pipe smoke is usually reported, related to someone who worked there.

Old, Large Homes and Buildings

Like most ancient castles, many very old, large buildings have ghosts. In an older home, a woman who lived there lingers to be sure that the house and its occupants remain safe. She usually wears a green dress.

Another ghost is mad and lurks in the attic, basement, or an outbuilding. A variation on this is a ghost in the nearby woods or a field next to an old homestead. These hauntings are almost predictable.

Old Hotels

Many hotels are haunted by the same people who visited them in life. They're usually happy ghosts who return to relax and enjoy themselves.

Classic haunted spots in hotels include the top floor, the elevator, and the lobby. This is true of the Driskill Hotel, Austin's most haunted and elegant hotel, and a favorite destination for visiting ghost hunters.

Around Austin, this category of haunting extends to former brothels. In the late nineteenth century, dozens of feisty, independent-minded madams owned "boarding houses" around downtown Austin. Today, these sites are often clubs, bars, and restaurants in the entertainment and warehouse districts of Austin. And, most of them have great ghost stories to share.

Hospitals, Retirement Homes, Morgues and Funeral Parlors

As you'd expect, some people aren't willing to leave the last place where they were seen and called by name. However, if these sites are still in use, they're usually off-limits to ghost hunters.

Instead, look for former locations of these kinds of buildings. They're usually haunted by perplexed and sometimes angry ghosts.

Around Austin, there are probably hundreds of unreported ghosts. If you follow these suggestions, you'll find even more ghosts than are included in these pages.

Guide for Urban Exploration

The following guide by Scott Lefebvre is from his book, Spooky Creepy Long Island. *It is used here with his permission.*

If you're anything like me, creepy looking abandoned buildings have an almost irresistible attraction as destinations for adventurous excursions.

Attractive destinations include abandoned buildings, usually the older the better, and especially asylums and churches, ex-military bases, and anything else interesting and off limits.

Many urban explorers bring back small souvenirs from their excursions. I still have two coffee mugs from the Ladd Center, which are precious to me. But I ask that if you do decide to visit someplace with the purpose of exploring it, that you avoid the urge to destroy or vandalize anything while you're there. Please think about preserving the site for other explorers. Vandalism only serves to increase security surveillance or make the site more likely to face destruction as a safety hazard and a popular destination for unwanted visitors. It's perfectly acceptable to take as many pictures as you desire, but the best souvenir will be your memory of the experience.

Things to Bring With You

Light

If your planned destination is a building, day or night, you'll want to bring a **flashlight**. If you enter an abandoned building, there will most likely be rooms that do not have direct access to the outside and will be dark without artificial light. It's also important to always be able to see where you're planning on going. The most common injuries for urban explorers are tripping over something underfoot because they weren't watching where they were going, or hitting their head or getting cut by something hanging down from overhead.

My favorite flashlight is the Mag-Lite mini. It's more expensive than the one-use flashlights that you can buy at the register or get for free as a promotional item with a pack of batteries, but it's infinitely more reliable and durable. It will survive a few accidental drops onto concrete floors, and the bulbs are cheap and replaceable. The light it throws is bright and clear and adjustable, and it's relatively cheap, so it won't be a big deal if you drop it someplace that you can't easily retrieve it. It runs on double A's and gets pretty good battery life, but **make sure you bring spare batteries**. You don't want to be trapped in an unfamiliar, potentially dangerous environment with a handful of dead flashlight.

Photography

A **camera** with a good flash is also highly recommended. Digital cameras are lighter and often cheaper than film cameras and can take a lot of pictures without requiring the user to play around with loading in a new roll of film in a dusty, musty environment. Plus, if you have to run, you don't want a bulky film camera with a flash attachment bumping around. Some of the most common sad stories about urban exploration are about broken or lost film cameras. Don't be one of those people.

Hair

Tying back long hair and wearing a baseball hat is recommended. You don't want your hair to accidentally get snagged on something and get pulled out. If you're going to hit your head on something it's better to get your hat knocked off than to get a rusty cut. Additionally, a stray hair flashed in front of a camera lens is frequently mistaken for evidence of the presence of the supernatural. A common and embarrassing error, and easily avoidable with a little precaution.

Attire

Wear **sensible shoes**. Sneakers with thick, skid-proof soles, or even better, work boots. The floors of abandoned buildings are often cluttered with debris and filth and sometimes damp or flooded. Also keep in mind that you may have to avoid wild animals or other hazards, so please be smart and tie your shoes. But only run if you're outside. Even a familiar spot might have changed since the last time you were there. Running in an unfamiliar environment is easily the best way to accidentally and possibly seriously hurt yourself while urban exploring.

You may want to bring light **work gloves**. Not so much to avoid leaving fingerprints, but more because abandoned buildings can be dirty places. There are rusty ladders and stairwell handrails and the walls are usually moldy. Anywhere you put your hands you can pick up dirt and you don't want that kind of dirt in your eyes or mouth. It's better to get your glove snagged on something sharp instead of cutting your hand open.

Just For Your Health

And speaking of mold and dust, if you're predisposed to allergies, you may want to invest in a good **dust mask**. In some old buildings there's lead paint dust and asbestos. I'm not too worried about breathing in a little toxic dust, but some of you may not be so careless.

Legalities

As I've stated earlier, we all know that **trespassing is illegal**. If you're uncomfortable with possible legal involvement, there are many excellent places of supernatural interest that are perfectly legal to visit and explore.

It's important to keep in mind that even going onto property that is not public can be considered trespassing. If you enter an abandoned building, that can be considered illegal entry and trespassing. And if you had to do anything to a window or door to get into a building, it becomes breaking and entering.

On a final note, I implore you to not bring any **weapons** along with you while urban exploring. Having a small pocketknife or pocket multi-tool like a Swiss Army Knife or a Leatherman can be convenient and handy, especially if your hair or clothes get snagged and you have to cut yourself loose. But it's completely unnecessary to bring a big hunting knife, or even worse, a handgun, along for the trip. If you're looking for ghosts, a weapon won't do you any good against them. Having a weapon just makes it that much more likely that someone will accidentally get hurt, and being discovered while urban exploring just gets more complicated if you're running around with a samurai sword.

Please be smart, be safe, and send me a set of your awesome pictures.

Or even better, take me along on your next trip.

Bibliography

Barnett, Chris. "Getting Up-to-Date in Tom's Town". *Continental,* in flight magazine (June 2006).

Iorg, Emily. "Haunted UMKC: Epperson House". *University News* (October 28,2002).

Iorg, Emily. "Haunted KC: The Savoy Hotel". *University News* (October 27, 2003).

Marin, Matthew. "'Haunted' Hospital Restored to Livable Senior Living Community". *Multi-Housing News* (October, 3, 2007).

The Vaile Mansion. Independence, Missouri: The Vaile Victorian Society.

Website Resources:
www.bellroadbarn.com
www.cinematreasures.org
www.dnr.mo.gov
www.elmsresort.com
www.ericjames.org
www.experiencekc.com/truman.html
www.exspgschamber.com
www.fbi.gov/libref/historic/famcases/floyd/floyd.htm
www.ghostvigil.com
www.interment.net
www.jchs.org
www.jessejames.org
www.kansascitymenus.com/majesticsteakhouse
www.kchistory.org
www.kclibrary.org/guides/localhistory
www.LegendsofAmerica.com
www.longviewfoundation.org
www.millersparanormalresearch.com
www.moioof.com
www.nps.gov/history
www.rockkc.com
www.savoyhotel.net
www.uchskc.org
www.umkc.edu
www.unews.com
www.unionstation.org

Locations of the Stories

Downtown Kansas City, Missouri

University of Missouri-Kansas City

Northland

Kearney and Excelsior Springs

Liberty and Smithville

Southland

Eastern Jackson County